1

Library of Congress Cataloging-in-Publication Data
Capozzoli, Christian

Improv | The Art of Collaboration / By Christian Capozzoli. - 1st ed.
ISBN - 979-8-3507-2966-5 (pbzk. : alk. paper)
1. Improvisation (Acting). 1. Title.

Editor: *Mary Ann Satter*
Illustrator: *Christian Capozzoli*
Layout and Typesetter: *Ubeyde Cimen*
Author Photo: *Sean Kara*

Production Service: *Upstate Litho*
Cover Design: *Ubeyde Cimen*
Cover Artwork provided by students, teachers and fellow performers from all over the world:
Eva Amaral, Jesko Bahr, Mia Barnes, Christian Capozzoli, Natascha Chada, Michael Churven, Ubeyde Cimen,
TJ Del Reno, Amanda Eid, Jon Kaplan, David Khuling, Gabi Köhler, Fiona Mallek, Veronika Olah, Anne Rab, Markus Rohr,
Mira Rohr, Albert Schimmel, and Joy Weeng.

IMPROV: THE ART OF COLLABO- RATION

ACKNOWLEDGMENTS

This book, from the front cover to the last page, was a collaborative effort. I have so many people to thank and credit for their time, talents, inspiration, and creativity.

I'd like to thank my mother and father, Rita and Louis Capozzoli, who impressed upon me the importance of hard work and loving what you do. Mary Ann Satter, my high school English teacher and editor of this book, who encouraged me to share the way I see the world. My wife, Joyce Kim for her love and support. My dear friend and designer of this book, Ubeyde Cimen.

I've been fortunate to train, work, and collaborate with improv legends and comedic directors: Mark Sutton, Mick Napier, Dan O'Connor, Randy Dixon, Charna Halpern, Julie Brister, John Lutz, Christina Gausas, Kevin Dorf, Armando Diaz, Kiel Kennedy, Jimmy Fowlie, Lauren Burns, Michael Churven, Rico Colindres, Lena Dunham, Robert Smigel, Adam Sandler, Stephen Colbert and David Gordon Green.

I'd like to thank every teammate of every team and cast I've been a part of at UCBTNY, Magnet Theater, Annoyance Brooklyn and Groundlings. A special thanks goes out to George Basil, Frank Campanella and Matt Evans. They were unflinchingly fearless, joyful and hilarious teammates and most of my matching techniques stem from the fun we had on stage together as 4TRACK.

There are so many schools and theaters to thank who have welcomed me as a performer, instructor, or as an academic strategist - Det Andre Teatret, Rapid Fire Theater, Dad's Garage, Second City, iO, Magnet Theater, UCB, Annoyance, RVAcomedy, the Whalefish Theater Collective, ImproNation, ImproTheater Mannheim, Spark, Grupa Ludzi, Teatro Breve, Der Kaktus, ITB, Copenhagen International Improv Festival, Wurzburger Improfestival, ImproFest Poland, Die Affirmative, Moment Fest, Carnegie Hall, Emerson College, Harvard University, Lesley University, Marymount Manhattan College, NYU, and Yale to name a very few.

I am inspired by and indebted to these incredible artists who have welcomed me in their communities and offered me fellowship throughout the years:

Helene Abrahamsen, Casey J. Adler, Clayton Aggeles, Kevin Ahart, Andrei Alupului, Eva Amaral, Nadine Antler, Russ Armstrong, Salome Attias, Maryam Azadi, Jesko Bahr, Jacob Banigan, Marianne Bayard, Claudia Behlendorf, Laura Berkemeyer, Josh Blubaugh, Rachel Bouton, Lena Breuer, Carolin Buchmann, Lisa Burnham, Matt Candio, Alistair Cook, Natalia Cyran, Dawn Dai, Emily Davis, TJ Del Reno, Markie Dinich, Amanda Eid, Gizem Erbas, Nicole Erichsen, Chris Frerichs, Camilla Frey, Tom Fischdick, Lena Forsch, Joanna Forys, Lilly Hartmann, Andrew Hefler, Tabea Herion, Kira Hess, Michal Iwanicki, Marian Janek Janusz, Jonathan Kaplan, Katarzyna Kasparek, Krysztof Kasparek, Tom Kelley, Judith Kirchgassner, Fleur Kläger, Adrian Klein, Susanne Konig, Nelli Kop, Gabi Köhler, David Kuhling, Lyndsi LaRose, Amanda Lazewska, Jim Libby, Brandon Lisy, Gunter Lösel, Susan Messing, Veslemoy Morkrid, Frank Odijk, Veronika Olah, Daniel Orrantia, Felipe Ortiz, Emily Pendergast, Liz Peters, Nils Petter Morland, Alan Pokosz, Anne Rab, Thom Roelofs, Markus Rohr, Mira Rohr, Hauke Scheer, Albert Schimmel, Lea Schubert, Carolina Sipos, Naomi Snieckus, Vid Sodnik, Sara Soukal, Cipha Sounds, Ann Kathrin Stengel, Claudia Stump, Kasia Szymanska, Andrew Wallace, Nele Weber, Taylor Dean White, Jens M. Wienand, Corbinian Wildmeister, Patrick Williams, Paul Ziehmer.

For the last twenty-four years, I have been unbelievably lucky to work with some of the funniest, most gifted, hilarious performers in the world. This book would not exist without the thousands of students, performers and instructors who have studied with me. Thank you. Your work, your trust and your sense of play inspired me to create some of these exercises and reimagine others to help improvisers cheer and champion each other on and off stage. Without these experiences, I would not have anything to share. For these opportunities, I am humbled and forever grateful.

CONTENTS

AN INVITATION TO COLLABORATE

This book is a seed. How we share it and who we share it with, helps it to bloom.

This is a living document.

Every doodle, every notion and note - twines, stretching, reaching to the next reader. Underlined and highlighted sections and dog-eared corners draw us in to dig further, find meaning and spur inspiration. Interact with this book, make it yours, leave your mark, question and prod, identify what irks you and fix it, find what's missing and add it, expand and explore using your genius.

Share this with people who would love the book, who would hate it, non-improvisers, artists, writers, performers who inspire you, who challenge you, whom you love to connect with or those that you wish you could connect with more.

Be open to connecting with what is there and what has been added. This is a collaboration. Share the process. The book should change every time it is shared. Don't be precious, or pressured to be profound — just be open and interested in connecting.

We need each other to grow this art form.
We need each other to grow.

Be brave, bring as much of yourself to this book as you can. The more you invest and share the deeper and more resonant and enriching it will become. Fill this book with you, your insights, your gifts, your viewpoints and education, your respect, reverence, love and wonder for this art form. Draw, comment, criticize, elaborate — fill the margins, and staple on pages to give your ideas the room they need. If we love improv, it's our responsibility to share what we know, show what it can be, and inspire it to be even more. That starts with sharing techniques, explaining our approaches, and offering them up to be used and improved upon to grow our communities stronger and push the art form further.

Every time you reread this book you will be different and it will be different because of you. Take the space, be part of the story and love what you share.

IMPROV EDUCATION

ART CLASS

An empty stage is full of possibility. It's easy to be dwarfed by its infinite potential. Swallowed by the nothing, drowning in everything. It intimidates. Some are stunned with preciousness; others swept up in a tidal wave of calculus and choices and games and rules, crippling imagination and ability to play, act and react. The stage is arrested, robbed of being or becoming anything at all.

In first grade, I had an art teacher, Mrs. Donovan. I loved her room stuffed full of artwork hanging by clothespins from wires. At the end of the day, the sun would pour in through tissue paper taped to the windows, like stained glass. One day she shared that she'd made paper for us and she wanted us to draw on it. Every kid got a piece; it wasn't construction paper; it wasn't just an 8 x 10 piece of white paper. It was special. It had little flecks of colors in it. What she'd done was take all the scrap pieces from the recycling bin, cut them up, wet them and mashed them into a pulp, rolled them out into new pieces of paper, then let them dry. They were beautiful. And I sat there in my corduroys staring at the blank paper while others scribbled and drew dinosaurs and houses. I just kept staring at my page empty, swallowed by all the things that could be. I didn't want to start anything because I was afraid of ruining and destroying something that was already beautiful.

When we watch an amazing improv set on stage, we idolize it, exalt the work, and the stage becomes an altar. We want to do work that can stand on the stage, not cheapen it. This is when anxiety creeps in, imposter syndrome rears its head, we overthink and stop playing, and stop being present.

I stared at that blank page for twenty minutes. Eventually, I was embarrassed just sitting there. Kids were finishing their pictures and Mrs. Donovan was on a ladder hanging them, and there I was locked up, stuck in the starting gate, paralyzed. And then I got judge-y, looking up at the pictures. Three of them looked identical: the same house, the same tree, the same smiling sun.

That's not art!

I was putting my creative energy into criticizing other work instead of doing the work myself.

Mrs. Donovan came by and touched my shoulder and asked why I hadn't started. I didn't have any words. I started to tear up and then she grabbed a magic marker, a purple one, she popped off the top and scribbled across the page and then handed me the marker and said **Finish it**. Then I dove in! The pressure of making something perfect went away. I wasn't trying to make something beautiful, I was trying to make something matter.

An improviser's brain loves to justify. In order to justify we need something deliberate, something declarative to create context and dimension around it. When we don't have a declaration or a starting point, we spin our wheels overwhelmed by everything. When we have everything, it's the same as having nothing. We need to make a simple choice; it can be anything, as long as it's something. Without a grain of sand, there would be no pearls.

Everything starts with something.

We have to risk ruining the page, being foolish, being wrong, making something derivative or hack. We have to not be so precious and trust that as long as we are engaging, trying, and dialoguing with the process instead of stuck on which word to use first, we will get better. We will learn to rely on ourselves and our abilities. We will surprise ourselves. It's unrealistic and unfair to ourselves and our scene partners to demand perfection without giving room to fail or to create and experiment.

> *Improv is the art of making things matter,*
> *through collaboration, imagination,*
> *justification and celebration.*

When you find yourself on the backline swallowed in a sea of possibility and hesitation, crying in your corduroys, don't worry about thinking of the perfect thing — just do something. Be fearless. Make choices that arrest the audience, not the stage. Be playful, bold, and unpredictable. And then, as a team, grow it, give it weight, and make it matter.

BLAZE NEW PATHS

You're in the woods, hungry; you can take a known path that leads to a pear tree or walk aimlessly and hope to find something. What are you going to do?

Players are programmed by their success. An approach that leads to a desired result gets patterned and repeated as long as it's fruitful.

It's human nature to lean toward our tendencies. Over time these choices and paths become us. Eventually, it's difficult to make any other choice. This is the trouble spot. This is why people have a hard time changing and trying new things.

We have to rewire ourselves for success, and break those patterns, instead of repeating and reinforcing them. If we only cling to the familiar, to our habits, to stability, we won't find anything new in ourselves. Every day will be pears. We won't surprise ourselves or the audience.

Improv needs risk. It needs danger. It needs us to embrace the unknown, and break out of our shells and ruts to make new neural pathways that will unlock ourselves from ourselves.

When we find ourselves wanting control, wanting to make things feel comfortable and familiar, we need to remind ourselves that that's just our ego, grabbing white-knuckled to our old self. We need to give ourselves permission to experience scenes and see ourselves from a new perspective. An improv education is an invitation for us to be brave, to try new things, to fail, to learn and grow. That's the aim.

Break old patterns to find new fruit.

I've spent nearly twenty thousand hours teaching improv. I've been honored to work with improv schools all over the world to reimagine their curricula. This begins with identifying the ethos of their theater and then designing lessons that tether to those core values, so all roads lead to Rome, so every class, course, and level has continuity. Beyond what is taught, we discuss how it is taught, devising shared language, metaphors, and principles to leverage learning. We scaffold lessons with deliberate aims to help students be better listeners and teammates. We create a safe and playful atmosphere where they

Improv: The Art Of Collaboration

can dare to be stupid, goofy and wrong and rejoice in their choices. We invite them to blaze new paths, to try new things, and to free themselves from themselves.

Note: Many of the exercises, drills and formats included in this book I learned from teachers I had throughout the years. Some are old standards and others are hybrids of pre-existing exercises. Unfortunately, there isn't an exact way to trace them back to a single person to give proper credit. My hope in including them here is to spotlight exercises and show how they can be scaffolded to devise lesson plans. Beyond their simple mechanics, I've tried to share the trappings of these drills and tweaks that can be made to enhance and refine their effectiveness. Please take, play and experiment with these exercises and formats to create new lessons of your own.

WRANGLING THE ROOM

Just before the very first class begins, there is a nervous thrum of energies in the room: some students are eager to hop up, others terrified, some stretch, others breathe actorly, a loud person forces jokes and laughs at themself, someone lost in work wraps up emails, another texts about brunch plans, while one grips their notebook tightly.

This is high-dive energy. The students have signed up for the class, committed, their toes are on the edge of the platform. The room swirls with fight-or-flight impulses, a frenzy of fear and excitement. They are about to do something that terrifies them and unlike the high-dive, they don't know what they're jumping into.

It is the instructor's job to wrangle all these varied energies in the room to create harmony and focus. Enter the room with earnest joy and enthusiasm. Don't bring your own anxiety or baggage, that will only add static to the room's noise. Enter with authority and intentionality. Wrangle the room. Invite them to hop up and get in a circle where they can all see each other. Corral the energies; help them be present and put a value on look-ing and connecting with each other.

I was asked to sub for a coach, last minute. I rushed across town to the room a few minutes late. People were still on their phones when I arrived. I apologized and asked them to circle up. I had everyone say their names and share a note they were currently working on. When they share personal issues they are working on, I devise a rehearsal to pinpoint those. This way if the issue happens once, I can call it out straight away.

> **Side Note:** When coaching, I don't give a note until I see something happen three times. Trying to note everything at all times can make the rehearsals overwhelming. If it's a mistake or just some rust, the behavior will correct itself. If it happens a second or third time in a three-hour rehearsal, then it's definitely worth noting.

Halfway around the circle, a person said their name, then explained that they were coaching this group. In my rush to get across town, I didn't see that the coach I was cov-ering for had found someone else. Instead, I stormed into a class and commandeered it like a pirate and everyone just followed along. People want to spend their money wisely. They want to be treated with care and attention. Even the other coach made a joke and said the thing they are working on is to not waste so much time before getting started with rehearsals.

Enter the room eager to work. Every minute matters, so make use of the time we're choosing to spend together to hone our craft and skill.

I start classes a minute early, inviting people to pair off and warm up their voices by sharing details about themselves while moving around. When students arrive and sit quietly, they are unintentionally ritualizing the space. The instruction to inhabit the space activates the room.

Those who are late arrive to a room that's already humming. This sends a subcon-scious message to the student:

> **This class will not wait for me.**
> **This class is all business when it comes to celebrating each other.**
> **I need to be on time because I don't want to miss out on something**

Improv: The Art Of Collaboration

When a teacher waits until everyone is present, that sends the opposite message:

> **We will wait for one person.**
> **We will not move forward.**
> **We will kill time.**

The teacher sets the tone. When a rehearsal lacks order and design, it fosters laziness, a bad work ethic, shrugs accountability, and diminishes the importance of even being there.

The rehearsal space itself should be neat and organized. A coach is paid to be aware, to see what's wrong and fix it. The students must trust that a coach will recognize when something is out of whack. If a trash can is overflowing, empty it. If condensation is dripping from the AC making a puddle in the middle of the room, mop it up. If yoga mats are slopped in a corner and the chairs are a mess, tidy up. Bring order to the room to create a safe and welcoming space to play.

Instructors build trust in the room through respect and support. They celebrate all perspectives. They foster camaraderie and a feeling of family to create a safe, empathetic space so teammates feel empowered to address any pre-existing triggers or traumas. This creates room for each player to be heard and their sensitivities to be shared while maintaining a spirit of adventure instead of a taboo minefield full of triggers and emotional shrapnel.

Instructors should set ground rules for the class and then invite everyone to share anything that will make them feel more comfortable, understood, heard and supported. It is each player's responsibility to communicate their boundaries to the class so that the class is aware and can then be respectful of those boundaries.

> *I have a bad back so please don't jump on me.*
>
> *In scenes, I'm up for playing any gender but when we host as ourselves before the show, I prefer they/them pronouns.*
>
> *I am in a classroom with third graders all day. I'd really prefer not to be labeled a teacher.*

It is the individual's job to maintain their own boundaries. They can set it and choose to cross it, adhere to it, or at any time call time out to remove themselves from a scenario in which they feel uncomfortable. The class will support their teammate with zero judgment and appreciate them for taking accountability for themself. A player does not set the rule for the class. They cannot expect everyone else to maintain their boundary for them but once informed the class will be understanding and sensitive to these boundaries and help to maintain them. For instance, if a player alerts the group that they have bad knees, it is their responsibility to make choices on stage that protect themself. If a scene involves a fire and everyone is crawling to avoid the smoke, it is their choice to join on the ground and wince through the pain, or stand up and remove themselves from the scene or become the flames enveloping a building.

When training teachers, I start having them present a *How To* tutorial for a very basic task like tying your shoes. A volunteer will leave the room, then I prompt the class to act a certain way when they re-enter. They are asked to be super chatty, collecting dues, or lackadaisical. The trainee's job is to enter with energy, take a quick read of the room, neutralize whatever rogue element is at play, get everyone up and looking at each other, and then clearly platform and share their mini-lesson.

Anxiety, nerves and imposter syndrome can rattle and complicate this straightforward task. First-time teachers will focus on their aim and miss small things scattered around the room. They aren't present. They're in their head. They might not even realize a chair is turned over on its side and needs straightening. They cling to their lesson without reading the room or taking in the students and the culture. Teachers need to be able to zoom in and out, in service of the students and ensemble, while creating a safe space to experiment and deliver their lesson plan.

SCAFFOLDING A LESSON PLAN

Every rehearsal should have an aim, a topic that is introduced as a framing device for the class and all notes should address that aim.

When I was in fifth grade, we had a take-home test. The assignment was to read the start of a story about a kid who is awakened from sleep by a magic carpet rapping at the window. We were to finish the story overnight. I wrote eight pages full of caves, treasure, barbarians, and an evil sultan who controlled scarabs with his mind. I was proud of my story. The teacher even read it out loud to the class, and I got a D.

The assignment was a reason to have us write, not to judge our creativity but to grade our grammar and spelling. This was unclear. Nowhere on the prompt did it say we'd be graded on punctuation. Some kids wrote ten perfect sentences and got an A.

When teachers set a lesson plan and an aim, it helps the students shoot at the same target, isolate a certain skill or tool, and keep things clear.

Of course, if something is extraordinarily good, take the time to underline its greatness, then get back to the aim.

All notes should fortify the lesson, and each lesson should reinforce the overarching game plan of the course. This takes planning.

Lesson Plan Template

TROUBLE SPOT	*Identify a team's weaknesses, anemias, bad habits or panic moves.*
THE AIM	*Isolate a clear improv goal or target for the lesson based on these trouble spots.*
EXTENDED METAPHOR	*Platform the lesson with an Anecdote or Metaphor.*
TAKE-AWAY PHRASES	*Establish two or three playful phrases that address the aim and the metaphor.*
DESIGNING LESSON	*Brainstorm possible warm-ups, scene drills, and exercises to address the aim.*
WARM-UPS	*Choose two to three warm-ups that explore the aim from different angles.*
SCENE DRILLS	*Choose Scene drills that dovetail from warm-ups and fortify the aim.*
EXERCISES	*Choose a scene exercise that dovetails from the scene drills.*
MINI-PIECES	*Assign a mini-piece as a means to explore and note the aim.*

AN EXAMPLE OF A LESSON PLAN:

Trouble Spot: A team is inventing more than they are investing.

The Aim: Illustrate the importance of unpacking declarations.

The Extended Metaphor/Anecdote: The immediate metaphor that comes to mind is pretty literal: When I was growing up, my family would drive a blind woman to church. My voice hadn't cracked, so she thought that my sister and I were both girls, Chrissy and Nikki. That Christmas she got us both matching silk pajamas that had turquoise and pink piping and wooden toggles. I loved it. I felt like the karate kid. Christmas morning my parents had the camcorder set on a tripod framing the tree surrounded with more gifts than any kids deserve. The tripod panned to the stairwell and you could hear our voices asking if we could come down. Then we ran into the living room. I started showing off my karate moves, and my sister was begging to open her gifts. Our parents nodded and we just tore into the tree. We'd pick up a present, rip it open just far enough to see what was inside, then throw the box and move to the next. We were feral. We were unhinged, grabbing ripping and throwing. My mom was yelling in the background, *Stop. No! Those aren't yours!* Within two minutes, it was over. Everything was open and my sister was on the tape dead center, crying, saying, *What's mine? What's mine?*

This is not a shining moment. We were spoiled brats. But we can learn from these embarrassments. There was a ton of love under that tree, tons of gifts waiting to be unpacked, but we didn't build a Christmas any of us are proud of. We sped past any opportunities to unpack the gifts. There was no chance to celebrate and adore and be gracious and thankful for our gifts. There was no horizon, just a tumultuous sea of wrapping paper and confusion. This is a bad improv scene: tons of gifts being missed, being ignored, being forgotten. No one feels loved, no one is listening, and no one knows what they have. Every offer misses their mark. Don't rush through Christmas. The audience watches us on stage unpack gifts with each other, so make sure that they know that those gifts aren't for nothing, that they are important, that they do matter to us, that they have significance, and that there is love in the room.

Let's re-think that Christmas in a healthy way. A single gift is pulled from under the tree, you read whose name it goes to and who it's from, you present it to them and all eyes lean in interested. They **OOH** and comment about the wrapping paper. They begin unwrapping it guessing at what it might be. They see where the box is from and say, ***You shouldn't have***. They open it and dig past the tissue paper to reveal the gift. They ooh and ahh at the gift. They are touched and moved by it. They are thankful and say kind words and hug the person who gave it to them. And that person lovingly explains why they gave it to them. Then they hold up the gift and pose for a picture. This shows the love we have not only for each other but for the importance of the gifts that are under the tree. In an improv scene, we want all that texture; one gift gives us all that mileage, a whole range of emotions, and a reason to celebrate.

Descriptive metaphors, like this, activate a different part of the brain and the recall is much sharper because it has narrative resonance. A year from now you can say the same phrase and plug into the same note. Some teachers may choose to give that long expla-nation at the very top or just share it in the first hour when it feels natural.

Take-Away Phrases: *Don't rush Christmas; Unpack the gift; Show the love; The present is a gift for us to unpack together*

Designing Your Lesson: *Gifts can be unpacked emotionally, narratively or with specificity.*

The warm-ups, drills and scene exercises should scaffold and reinforce this statement. Scene work then dovetails to Mini-pieces that are noted with this lens as well. This gives the lesson a coherent arc. A great teacher tailors their lessons to meet the exact needs of the group based on their strengths and anemias.

WARM-UP 1:
THE GRACIOUS GOAT

Begin with everybody in a circle. One player gestures that they are holding a small goat. They cross extending the goat to another player and say,

> *I give you the gracious goat.*

The receiving player accepts the goat and responds,

I have the gracious goat.

Those to the right and left of the receiving player lock eyes like towns person one and two in *Beauty and the Beast* and rejoice,

They have the gracious goat!

Then the two players to their side drop to a knee and exclaim,

Isn't it grand to have the gracious goat!!

Then the receiving player crosses and extends the goat to another prompting the same avalanche of enthusiasm.

Push the players to say these flat phrases with elation and earnestness. Help them see when it feels phony or trite. An improv goat may seem stupid but it is only made more stupid and less important when players snub the gift. Stress that they revel in the gift, feel the weight of the goat, make it real and make it matter. Each phrase is meant to amplify the sentiment through celebration, each declaration more exuberant.

Warm-ups deserve notes. Just because a group masters the warm-up doesn't mean they understand it. Take the time to frame how it incorporates and addresses the aim. In this case, one *AND* or gift is unpacked three times with *YES* and *OOH* before another *AND* is shared. This serves to slow down Christmas and fill it with meaning and importance.

When the group excels and is hitting the target, let them know, and challenge them with a more sophisticated twist on the warm-up to build confidence and morale. For instance, brainstorm ways people might feel when receiving a gift: embarrassed, happy, sad, angry, let down, intimidated, shy, scared.

Now have everyone choose one of these words and hold it in their heart. When the goat is given to them they will tap into this feeling and say the same lines, only this time infused with the sentiment they chose, radiating the emotion (fear) to the rest of the circle. The players to the right and left will echo and heighten the fear into fright. Although the lines stay the same, the tone amplifies and unpacks the terror. Finally, two players drop to a knee and name the sentiment by declaring,

Isn't it scary to have the gracious goat!

If players use the same words to define the sentiment, amazing. If they use synonyms, great. But if they both fail to pick up on the sentiment, note it right away. This usually stems from the receiving player swallowing their choice which cloaks the sentiment and prevents others from identifying, aligning and bolding that choice.

This exercise illustrates the emotional power a single offer can yield when it is unpacked. If this much joy or fear can be drawn from an invisible goat, it can be done with any offer. Even a sneeze can be rallied around and unpacked. If the sneeze is first received with concern:

Oh, don't tell me you're sick!

Then the people next to them will amplify that concern.

My god, you came to work sick!

Then even more agitated.

You don't think of anyone but yourself. You are a disease on this office.

Instructors shouldn't speed through warm-ups to honor their own agenda. Work at the pace of the room and repeat the warm-up until the aim and the lesson seem to be second nature.

Emphasize how unpacking a single offer generated so much joy. If they were just handing a goat back and forth without any unpacking, the warm-up would feel robotic and uninspired. Any sound, glance, or object can be unpacked in this same way.

After that warm-up, have everybody take a seat. Directing them to sit and stand to move from one part of the room to another allows the instructor to conduct the energies of the room. Don't let students stand or sit in the same place for too long. Students gauge their improv class based on this metric.

Improv: The Art Of Collaboration

STUDENT: *That class was awful. I only got up once in three hours.*

Knowing this, get them up and moving around the room often. If they have a moment of failure let them move through it. Don't let them stand in that failure for too long eroding their self-confidence. If they zone out, shake things up, and refresh the room so that they don't stagnate. This allows them to see the room and the exercise from a new angle.

WARM-UP 2:
WOW, WHAT A GREAT WEDDING

INSTRUCTOR: *Let's get six brave people up on stage!*

When introducing an exercise, you don't always have to leave it up to chance. They may be brave but it doesn't mean they are good. Sometimes it's better to just select six.

INSTRUCTOR: *You six, jump on up.*

This allows the instructor to hand-pick players who are best suited to the exercise, it saves time and betters the odds of effectively platforming the exercise for everyone.

Wow, What A Great Wedding begins with a player stepping forward with the declaration, *I'm getting married!*

Everyone cheers for them.

ALEX: *And you're all invited!*

Everyone cheers again, more enthusiastic as Alex hands out invitations.

ALEX: *As you can see it's a theme wedding ...*

Then they name the theme, *Pixar, Christopher Nolan films, Video Games,* etc. Encourage it not to be too obscure like medieval Portuguese literature.The idea is not to stump our scene partners but to create a playground at the crossroads of these two vectors, where we can marry wedding specifics and theme specifics.

> ALEX: *And the theme is Greek mythology!*

Immediately someone in the circle needs to justify why Greek mythology:

> JAMIE: *Oh, because you and Tad met while doing a semester abroad in Athens!*
> ROWAN: *And you love Moussaka and Souvlaki!*
> DRU: *And isn't your Dad half Greek?!*

These justifications are great, but offer after offer, gift after gift, nothing is being unpacked. They are *Rushing through Christmas*. Let it happen. Let them fail and be there to help frame those failures and learn from them. Explain how the Gracious Goat is a more emotional warm-up, whereas this is more cerebral and premise-based. It puts them in their heads, *AND*-ing. Everyone gets so excited to say their idea that no one takes time to react to other people's ideas. They become *AND*-ing machines. We wind up with a glorified list of offers with no detail, emotion or play. None of our offers matter if we chuck them aside and replace them immediately with new ones that also don't matter.

Players may understand the note intellectually but that does not mean it's in their muscle memory. Take the time to unpack each offer. It communicates to the audience that it matters, that we are reacting and being affected by each other and our gifts. Delight in the information they have, volleying it, reflecting on it, unpacking with details.

> JAMIE: *Oh, because you and Tad met while doing a semester abroad in Athens!*
> ROWAN: *How romantic!*
> DRU: *It's crazy. And remember you didn't even want to do that trip.*
> ALEX: *I know!*
> ROWAN: *But I guess Aphrodite and the Fates had different plans for you two.*

Then moving on, to the next wedding idea that relates to Greek mythology.

> DRU: *Ooh, speaking of Aphrodite, you should emerge from a clam shell in your wedding dress.*
> ALEX: *That would be everything.*
> JAMIE: *Gorgeous!*
> ROWAN: *You're going to look like an absolute goddess.*

Rejoice in every choice, and respond to it earnestly before making the next offer.

> JAMIE: *Oh, Oh, and instead of a ring bearer, dress him up as cupid with wings.*
> ALEX: *That's precious. I love that.*
> DRU: *I love your love!*

Unpacking, nourishes scenes with emotion, texture and opinions.

> JAMIE: *And instead of a limousine. You can have a chariot …*
> ROWAN: *Made of obsidian pulled by black horses.*
> DRU: *Like when Hades emerged from the underworld for his bride Persephone.*
> JAMIE: *That way you don't have to rent a big old smelly limousine.*
> ALEX: *I love the idea of a green wedding. And you know who else would love that?*
> ALL PLAYERS: *Demeter!*

These warm-ups ramp into scene drills focused on the same aim of Unpacking. Remind the class of this aim and encourage them to carry the notes with them into the next drill.

SCENE DRILL:
NO, YOU DIDN'T

Begin splitting the class in half, forming two drill lines facing each other, A and B. A presents B with a gift and initiates with a line of dialogue. B receives the gift with the phrase *No, you didn't* and unpacks the offer through a predetermined lens, similar to the Gracious Goat warm-up.

Always use a canned example to platform an exercise. This ensures a clear model for the drill and saves time.

Player A thinks of a gift in their mind: Ice Cream.
Player B thinks of a predetermined sentiment: Trying to have willpower.

> PLAYER A : *I got you this ice cream cone.*
> PLAYER B: ***No, you didn't*** *… Thank you, but I can't. I already had two cheat days this week. It is calling my name but I'm strong, I don't need … Is that Pistachio?*

Player A is permitted to add detail. Player B will unpack it with the same emotional stance.

> PLAYER A: *Yep, and apparently the pistachios were imported from Sicily.*
> PLAYER B: *My goodness, I want to be good but that green is just saying go for it! I can be good when I'm dead and gone. You only live once! No, no, I can't. I can't see myself as a cheater. I know, blindfold me with your scarf and give me that cone.*

Next, everyone at the same time, drills these four-line scenes with their partner. Running drills this way is super efficient. In less than six minutes the entire class gets two to four reps. It's the improv equivalent of giving everyone in gym class a basketball to shoot around and work on their shot.

In a bustling crowd, there is a certain level of anonymity. It allows students to try out the exercise in private before needing to perform for the class. They can focus on the mechanics while the teacher moves around the room listening in on different exchanges and helping those that are struggling.

After everyone does the exercise twice, give quick pointed notes. Make sure to call out successes. Be detailed. Quote the scenes you overheard and underline how Unpacking provided traction and power.

Spotlighting certain exchanges and using direct quotes lets students know that the instructor is always watching and listening, even when they feel invisible in the room.

Sixteen people doing this exercise one by one would take roughly twenty-five minutes. Everybody doing it at once only takes five. These reps are invaluable. Doing something once you succeed or fail, but giving the opportunity to try three times, allows for corrections to be made, familiarity to be gained, and the lesson to resonate.

After a full round, ask the class to cite and recall *Unpacking moves* that were particularly funny or effective. This builds ensemble. Students have to be fans of each other not just of themself. When students highlight good work, it builds camaraderie, admiration and trust for one another. Instructors should reserve sharing their opinions until after students have shared theirs. Better yet, cosign student observations and expand on them to get to the aim of the lesson.

Now, invite eight people up to form sidelines four on each side. Students rarely want to be the first. Even if nobody is getting up, start to count as though they are, *Great, we've got one, two, three …*

Improv: The Art Of Collaboration

When students hear others are jumping up, even if they're not, it creates momentum in the room and they'll hop up.

Players on stage right will play the A role presenting a gift. Players on stage left will play the B role by reacting to the gift with a predetermined stance. These begin the same way as the previous drill only now the scene is given more time to heighten and explore.

Side Note: I prefer to leave the sidelines loose, meaning any A can initiate the next scene and any B can receive their gift. This creates a more fluid *show-like* environment and allows players to follow their feet, based on impulse and inspiration, instead of marching in line. Other teachers prefer to create a queue, A1 initiates for B1, A2:B2, etc. I think this can rattle students making them more anxious. That panic clouds the exercise; students start pre-planning, counting to figure out who they'll match with which takes them out of the assignment. However, if the aim of a class was confidence and geared at not cracking under pressure, then I would create a queue and traps for the players to amp up their anxiety levels and make them feel watched and claustrophobic, to work through these feelings and still deliver.

Call these scenes on the quick side. None should last more than a minute. As the scenes end, the players switch sides.

Before a scene exercise begins, encourage the class to engage and support the players.

INSTRUCTOR: *Let's give them some love!*

This invites the audience to invest, laugh and lean into the scenes and establishes respect for the work and the players doing the work.

INSTRUCTOR: *We benefit from their successes and mistakes. Let's give them our focus and energy, so they can feed off it. So they can do their best, so we can do ours.*

Performers want to connect with an audience, be heard, be seen, and be understood. When we give them that, and they feel the *love*, it empowers them to be bold. I note the first three scenes heavily. By making a practice of this, players will associate going early with getting more direct notes and attention. I call out what I love and try to make sure that anything that wobbles is noted right away so that bad habits don't get patterned.

INSTRUCTOR: *These notes are for the entire room. Let's not waste each other's time by having me repeat them. Each scene should be learning from the last scene, building off our collective successes and failures to grow.*

Towards the end of the exercise, most notes have been said and reiterated, so there's a shared shorthand that keeps the notes snappy.

EXERCISE: **ZHUZHING**

Next, we move to an exercise that involves teasing and zhuzhing a gift, paraphrasing and sharing sentiment to the nth degree. This drives home the importance of endorsing each other's moves. We slow Christmas down by trading in speed for fullness.

Begin with everybody in a circle. One person steps forward to offer a character spine and statement.

FRANK: *I want extra cream cheese, but not if it's extra.*

Now someone paraphrases this sentence by putting it in their own words while channelling the character.

MATT: *I want additional dairy spread, but not if it's going to cost me!*

Now another paraphrases the sentence again.

GEORGE: *Yeah, and I want more of that delicious creamy thick milk, but I'm not paying a penny more.*

Paraphrasing is like teasing your hair, you grab a section zhuzhing it so that it gets fuller. You're not adding any new hair, you're just giving what you have volume. As we paraphrase the statement, it gets more pronounced to a point of absurdity. It's full of texture, nuance, and characterization because we took the time to unpack the offer. Challenge the room to unpack and tease out the offer as many times as they can without adding anything new. Often players want to outwit the last witticism but sputter out trying to sound smart. If they are putting this pressure on themselves, invite them to any it dumber not smarter. *Creamy Thick Milk* is dumb and fun and keeps the tempo going.

SCENE EXERCISE:
OBJECTS & OPINIONS

Unpacking as an improv concept gives us surface area, texture, and detail; it awakens our environment and helps us use it as kindling for our scene. Sometimes there are only three gifts under the tree, but that's all a scene needs if we unpack Christmas correctly.

Begin by having everyone take out their phones. Ask them to make an honest list of things they need from the grocery store. Give them a full minute to jot these down, then ask them to include a few items they'd just love to have, like chocolate-covered espresso beans, a pint of ice cream or salt and vinegar potato chips.

Now place two chairs in the center of the room and invite two volunteers to take a seat with their phones.

Instruct one player to share something from their list. Their scene partner will immediately blurt out a detailed opinion about that item and then the first player will share their opinion.

Example:

> NAOMI: *Golden Pineapple Kombucha.*
> BEN: *Gross. I know it's good for gut health. But, eww, it just makes me gag.*
> NAOMI: *Oh, see, I love it. It's got a teensy bit of alcohol which makes every day a boozy brunch day.*

Now Ben will share an item from his list.

Example:

> BEN: *Zip Ties.*
> NAOMI: *I actually hate them. I know they are very useful but they legit give me nightmares.*
> BEN: *I hear you but the cords behind my TV look like a snake pit. I need order in my life.*

Underline just how much information we unpacked from these two items. Everything we touch gives us information, revelations, and opinions. Our truthful responses bring authenticity and realism to our characters. Every item has a story to tell.

Now, invite two players to begin a scene using these unpacking techniques in a location unrelated to their grocery list. The goal is to visualize their environment and interact with objects. Their declarations will paint the scene, and their opinions will inform their characterization.

Example: Kitchen

> CLAIRE: *Is this hot plate hand-drawn? It's beautiful.*
> Ezra: *Yeah, isn't it? My mother's aunt up in BC made it. She's 91. Can you believe that?*
> CLAIRE: *It's gorgeous. Look at the horsetails and hydrangeas and lavender.*
> EZRA: *I know, but then Jake, my brother-in-law, dropped it. If you look you can …*
> CLAIRE: *I can see the crack.*
> EZRA: *Now, I only bring it down for special occasions with civilized company.*

This is both a lesson in unpacking and visualization. We need to learn to use our words to create objects and dimension for the audience. We must help the audience use their imagination to see our imagination. Any object we touch should be unpacked with importance. It takes a lot of brain power to visualize these things, when we do we need to get as much juice out of it. You don't just squeeze an orange once and move on to the next, wring, twist and squeeze it dry, then move on.

Example: Arcade

Players stand slack-jawed looking at the Killer Instinct cabinet a 2D-fighting game. They see gum stuck under the console. They scoff, shaking their heads. One pulls a chisel from their belt. When one player holds the chisel, they find blisters on their palms, and when they look at the blisters they see old scars or Band-Aids on their hand. In half a second, all of this texture and specificity unfurls from this simple wad of gum. They get down on their knees and tilt their head to scrape the gum off the underside of the console.

> TAYLOR: *Swear to God, I see one of those greasy, rat-faced little twerps with gum in here again.*
> RUSS: *Oh I know, last Thursday I went home and I had grape gum all up in my hair.*
> TAYLOR: *That's it. I'm gonna take this chisel and go full Rambo mode on them.*

This is a great exercise for players who are talking heads in their scenes, haunting their environments and unable to interact with anything. If you point at it, cross to it, pick it up, be affected by it.

Next, have two players begin a scene. This time any object, they create in the environment, must at the very least yield two opinions before moving on to something else.

> # *A genie's lamp and all its wishes,*
> # *secrets and power*
> # *is just a lamp if you don't rub it.*

Example: AirBnB

A player crosses to the window sill in the kitchen.

> AUBREY: *Oh look at these shot glasses with a little cactus on it for Palm Springs.*
> DEVIN: *Those are cute.*
> AUBREY: *Aren't they.*
> DEVIN: *Put it in your purse.*
> AUBREY: *What, no!*
> DEVIN: *We're paying enough for this AirBnB. They can afford it.*
> AUBREY: *I could never.*
> DEVIN: *Yes, you can. Here, open your purse.*
> AUBREY: *No. Every time I looked at them I'd feel like a thief.*

The first declaration states that the shot glasses are cute.
The second states they should steal them because they're paying a lot for their stay.
The third refuses to take them because they don't want to be a thief.

Unpacking the shot glasses yielded three opinions in nine lines of dialogue, and helped identify our characters through their behaviors and world view. Now the players can move around in their scene and find another item to discover new information or to grow the same game.

> AUBREY: *Oh look at this Palm Springs magnet on the fridge.*
> DEVIN: *That's even cuter. Open your purse.*
> AUBREY: *What, no! I'm not a thief.*

Listing objects without unpacking them is fruitless; all of a sudden you're in a prop closet instead of a scene. Take time to mine every item for all its potential. Make statements and declarations about these gifts, and know why they matter. If they matter to us, they will matter to the audience, and the audience will be drawn in by our creativity.

MINI-PIECES / FORMATS:

Next, invite the room to perform a mini-piece. Explain that they don't need to worry about doing great scene work. Instead, ask that they focus on incorporating the various unpacking techniques to make sure scenes have fullness. If the scenes happen to be wonderful, even better.

After the piece, the instructor can encourage positive feedback from those watching. This allows students to have a true appreciation for each other. They must develop language and the ability to recognize what they like in scenes and why they worked and not just parrot what the teacher thinks.

Highlight the Unpacking moments that hit the mark. It's not just what instructors say but how they say it. Word choice and terminology inspirit the room and set the tone of the class to create a safe, supportive environment. When giving notes be clear, and try to use language that cuts the academic pretension.

> **Note 1** - *Remember, we don't want to rush Christmas.*
> **Note 2** - *Again? You guys keep forgetting to unpack your choices.*

These both address the same note but the first uses *we* and references a past note from a shared lesson in a positive light. The second blames the team and distances the coach from the team. When notes are steeped in negativity, students feel inferior and shut down. Petrified, they cling to past successes out of fear of making new mistakes. Without trying new things, they become outdated, fossils of a one-trick pony.

Instructors must create an environment that celebrates risk/trial and error, experimentation, exploration and adventure. Cheer students to embrace mistakes and not fear them, praise them when they surprise themselves and fail spectacularly then help them recognize their errors and learn from them. Rewind and recall previous failings and notes of earlier scenes, and thank the players for those mistakes. Without them, we wouldn't have heard the notes, to reach this shared understanding that led to these successes. Framing failures in this positive way creates fearlessness in the students and allows everyone to feel part of the successes.

Notes are a form of love and investment. Treat everyone as professionals dedicated to growing as players. Help them hear their successes and failures and see where they can be more precise or absurd or committed.

Noting a piece should not last longer than the piece itself. You are an instructor, not a stenographer. Some newer coaches will write down every line of dialogue. They are so busy transcribing that they don't experience the scene as an audience.

You don't hire a tape recorder to make you a better jazz musician.

The team or class is paying for an instructor's expertise. They want pointed notes. They want to trust that their instructor understands scenes ten times better than they do. They are paying for an instructor's eyes, their attention to detail and their comedic taste.

When an expert watches a scene they see the show in bullet time. They don't just see the mistakes. They see the forensics, the moves before the moves that led to panic and broke the scene's confidence or connection. It takes incredible focus to be clocking everything, every line, every gift, everyone's eyes, every brushstroke, then zooming out to catch the broad strokes as well. When an instructor's face is in their notebook, they're missing most of that.

Apparently, the Beatles never wrote down their melodies. The thought behind this is that if the melodies were worth remembering they wouldn't need to be written down.

The same is true for notes. If it is jaw-droppingly good or supremely awful, chances are it'll stick with you long enough to note it.

As an instructor, your mug is bigger than your students, because the more you perform and teach the more the art form slows down for you. In those gaps and pauses, you'll see entire universes. You can only fill their mug so much before it overflows and they're staring at you drowning in the gobbledegook. The instructor needs to have a read of their students; How big is their mug? How much can they handle? They need to be able to calibrate their notes to the class's level. So that the notes can be effective, filled to the very top, but not a drop more. This requires selectivity. An instructor must prioritize which notes need to be addressed and which can wait.

> **Note:** If given notes are intentionally or unintentionally ignored by the team or player, continue to give the note at least two more times. Try rephrasing it for the player and the betterment of the whole ensemble. However, if someone is just incapable or unwilling to hear it or change, know when to stop. Don't allow one player's ineptitude or resistance to monopolize everyone's time.

WARM-UPS

Warm-ups should awaken the ensemble to celebrate each other. They establish a culture of yes, fertile soil where any silly seed of an idea can be planted and take root and grow because it is being celebrated and nourished with acceptance instead of judgment.

Not every warm-up works for every team. Each group has its anemias. Every city conditions people to put up different defenses to survive whether it's climate, culture or stress.

In New York City, it's all hustle, constantly thinking steps ahead, angling. There, you learn quickly not to make meaningful eye contact with strangers. It invites danger. No one wants to be stabbed, so they adopt this soft focus. But when New Yorkers come into an improv class without a proper warm-up, there's no connection.

Studies show that as we become more dependent on devices our vision is narrowing. A warm-up needs to reset our vision, get our heads on a swivel, open ourselves to taking in offers, and alert to subtle shifts in the room. The creative spirit needs to be there, egoless, eager, and ready to dive on any offer made.

Since the advent of social media, there is a weirdness about being looked at or sharing space in a room. Students feel uncomfortable and vulnerable. They're used to curating what people see, taking twenty pictures before posting *the one*, only putting their best foot forward with their favorite filter. They are guarded. Warm-ups are meant to break down the stuff society and technology are putting between us. Do not rush through them.

It's the instructor's job to get the gunk out of their eyes and help players see each other and be seen. Point the microphone to the speaker to create a feedback loop that catches every sound and offer. So players don't feel invisible in plain sight. This places importance and value on connectivity. When we are lost we need to look at each other to find the scene. Discoveries come from connection. Inventions are found alone, then we pitch ideas to our scene partners instead of playing them.

If a group becomes too proficient at a warm-up, it's no longer serving its purpose. They will autopilot and plateau. A warm-up should push a team's limits. Challenge ensembles to add speed or dimension that increases the difficulty level so they are sharpening their tools, building endurance, lifting five hundred so they can throw fifty.

The instructor needs to read the room and prescribe warm-ups that disarm these defenses, push the team's limits, and open players to create a state of flow between them.

ZOMBIE TAG

Begin with the ensemble forming a large circle, and explain that their feet must be kept planted in place. The instructor will then enter the circle becoming a classic foot-dragging George A. Romero zombie hungry for brains. The zombie will lock in on a player and slowly close in on them. The only recourse the player has is to divert the zombie to another player. They do this by making eye contact with anyone in the circle, then that player can shout any other player's name, and the zombie will then instantly shift to hunt the newly named player.

This warm-up is about having confidence in the face of danger by creating a key association that when players are in trouble, they need to look to their teammates and connect, have trust and faith in the ensemble, and work together to stave off any dread.

Players' eyes fill with horror. When people panic, their heart rate escalates, their vision narrows, and their equilibrium and listening are off. Fear overwhelms them as they seize and forget the rules. Let them work through this. Selfishness and self-preservation betray the ensemble, fracturing the team's focus and feeding their fear.

Remind the players that this is pretend. The zombie will not kill them. Zombies are not real. There is a difference between playing scared and actually being scared. Players must work as an ensemble to keep each other safe and keep the fear at bay. They must play with danger, show the risk, but not actually be frozen with fear.

As a zombie closes in on a target, players fall into this trap, the target locks eyes with a person directly across the room, and that person looks to the target's right or left and yells their name. This allows the zombie to sidestep and make an easy kill. Work smarter to steer the zombie. If the zombie is centered everyone is at the same risk, bait them toward their target, instead of shouting a name when a player receives eye contact wait til the last second then redirect the zombie back across the circle. This note emboldens the ensemble to play with danger instead of fear it. Soon players selflessly sacrifice themselves, shouting their own name to keep the zombie from their teammates.

As the ensemble becomes more adept at conducting the zombie, challenge them to eliminate any *Uhhs* or *Umms*. Invite the zombie to get incrementally faster with each redirect, until they are running amok. This keeps players' heads on a swivel, present and alert. If a zombie manages to reach a player, the zombie switches spots with them and the victim becomes the new zombie.

This warm-up is perfect for addressing how players manage fear. Anxiety takes hold of people on the backline. They tense up. The moment they leave the backline they take a breath as though they're about to plunge off a bluff into black water. They drop into the scene and continue to hold their breath underwater, subconsciously drowning in their fear, desperate to find a game. They kick and squirm, unable to think because they are unable to breathe.

> *Perceived danger can rattle*
> *our focus and*
> *make easy things hard.*

Don't suffocate yourself and your scene and let fear devour your brain. Perceived danger can rattle our focus and make easy things hard. Work together when this happens, connect with your teammates, trust in the ensemble and be selfless and supportive.

VOLLEYBALL

This warm-up activates both sides of our brain while keeping us on our toes and working together to create a cogent stage picture.

Begin by gesturing that there is an invisible net splitting the room, with half the class on one side and half on the other. Invite them to huddle up with their teams and get ready to play volleyball against each other. They will pass the improvised ball from person to person using each other's names. When serving the ball they'll yell a person's name on the other side of the net, and everyone else will trace the ball with their eyes as it moves through the air and lands at that person. That person will say another person's name as they bump the ball, volleying to them.

Allow the group some time to get used to the mechanics. Invite them to create the illusion of speed by working together. Once they have a handle on this and know each other's names, it is time to add to it.

The goal is not just to volley the ball around but instead to work as a team to score points. True to volleyball, a team can only score when they are serving and they cannot pass to more than two people on their side before having to send it to the other side of the net. Set these rules and play by them.

The instructor acts as the ref. They must be definitive in their calls. Demand that the teams stay engaged; if they hesitate too long or say *Uhh* or *Umm*, that's a dropped ball, resulting in a point for the serving team, or the ball goes to the other team to serve.

When teams score, encourage them to celebrate, get hyped and love each other. When the ball is dropped, have them bark at each other or give each other pep talks. Of course, this is all performative. Players should not take this personally. This is to help the ensemble work as a team to create dynamic, action-packed drama for the audience. The audience needs to believe the players care, that this is the state finals, that this is about their legacy. The more the players care and the more real they treat this invisible game, the more the audience will lose themselves and be drawn into their imagination. Players must show the pressure. But do this as characters and deep down know that there is only love for each other in the room. That way, egos don't get bruised even when the losing team gets annihilated.

Once they've established a proficiency for this, add to it. The serving team now dictates how many passes must be made before the ball can be sent back over the net. For instance, if a player says **Service One**, that means it will go from one side of the net to the other side of the net, back-and-forth until the point is scored. The next person to serve will dictate the new rhythm, **Service Two**, which means it will pass to the other side and then be passed to another teammate before being sent back over the net to the other team where it will pass to another person on their team before being sent back over the net.

The options are Service One, Service Two, or Service Three. This is where math and listening come into play. It requires tons of focus, physicality and group endorsement. Don't get caught up in the math, give over to it. Done correctly there are moments where audiences can see the volleyball because the players are so compelling in their move-ments that the ball forms in the audience's imagination. Teammates should be hungry to play together as they win or lose as a team.

In keeping score, play until a team gets to five points and wins by two.

To add a level of difficulty to the exercise, incorporate Service Wild. This prevents the players from using anyone's actual names. Instead, they create nicknames on the fly that begin with their teammate's real initials. Melissa Jenkins would receive the ball if someone said Marmalade Jam or MacBeth Jubilee.

SPOTLIGHT HYDRAULIC

With everyone in a large circle, the instructor raises their right arm bent at the elbow pointing at the ceiling. Everyone else points at the instructor's right elbow. The instructor with their raised arm is *The Interesting* and everyone else pointing at the right elbow is *The Interested*. Those are the two options: Interesting or Interested.

Now, the entire circle must act as a single hydraulic. For the Interesting's arm to go down someone else's arm must go up. This is done by the Interesting making deliberate eye contact with an Interested player in the circle, and as one resigns the other lifts up and like clockwork the Interested point at the new Interesting.

Allow them to move and play with this mechanic. Encourage them to add sound, speed and sharpness. In every moment, players are either in the spotlight or they are the spotlight. Teams must work together to help the audience see the spotlight and where to look.

This demands engagement. Great ensembles put a premium on engagement and celebrating each other.

Players should never be standing still waiting for their turn to be interesting. If we are not interested in each other, the audience will not be interested in us. Even worse, if players aren't patient and they fight for focus, talking over each other, because everyone is interesting and no one is interested, the audience winds up lost in the Where's Waldo mayhem, with everyone vying for the audience's attention but paying none to each other.

A large majority of the time players will be a cradling energy, framing the interesting, shining all their light on their teammates. But it is still paramount that players be ready to own the spotlight when it is their turn.

Normally, players understand this theoretically, but it's important to invite them to make more full-bodied choices. Now, the Interesting lifts both arms over their head to take focus. The Interested bow, kowtowing, their arms outstretched with jazz fingers, every ounce of energy exalting the Interesting with laser focus. This should be a workout. Challenge players to engage their core, humble themselves, and abandon their egos to lift up, support and worship each other. The hands of a clock get the most attention, but if every gear doesn't work in disciplined harmony, it's not time worth keeping.

This engagement is everything. On the backline for scenes, everyone should be this attuned, on their toes like infielders. Ready. Nimble. Twitchy. Active. Revere the scene, respect the people in it, and give them your focus and energy. Cradle and contextualize with walk-ons, or atmosphere, or simply by giving them space and using your energy to hold it for them.

COOEY COOEY COOEY

Begin by splitting the group to either side of the room. Invite a player to walk plainly from one end to the other. Self-conscious players will try to be weird with their walk to get a laugh. Note this right away. The walk doesn't need anything extra. It should be natural and real. Encourage the others to study the walk from start to finish.

For instance, the player may have taken a slight breath before they began. They may have led with their head and shuffled across the room at a quick pace.

Next, have someone mimic what they saw. It's tempting to over-exaggerate this. Urge them to be faithful to their observations. This is an exercise in realism and repetition. Don't force the funny. It needs to be earned.

Now have another mimic what they saw in the second player, and then another and so on. With each exchange, the walk becomes more pronounced. Without steering it to a whacky place there is a natural degradation or enhancement of the walk. The funny comes from underlining and bolding what's there. The slight breath becomes a full breath, a gulp of air, a giant gulp. They barrel forward with the crown of their head, charging across the room briskly.

Every choice can be traced back to the first walk. Nothing is invented. This is a celebration of behavior and investment through discovery and observation.

Scenes need truth. Realness and repetition lead to caricature, absurdity and commentary.

When we first learn cursive, it feels labored. The pencil sits snug in our fingers as we focus and struggle with each letter to sign our name. But through repetition, we find the fluidity of our signature, and that flow leads to flare, and that flare leads to flamboyance. A single line, a single walk becomes a rollercoaster, becomes an attitude, a viewpoint.

Now invite two people to match the flare, and another two to match them, then three, then four as it heightens to lunacy. As players move together across the room they must feed off each other. Whenever anyone joins your fun, acknowledge them as your twin, nod to them, and delight in the connection as a way of thanking them for digging on your idea.

COOEY CHAIR

Invite six players to stand on one side of the room and then place a chair in the center. Instruct a player to enter as a trailblazer. Their job is to create a sequence of events that incorporates the chair for the others to pattern.

They should enter the room with emotion and history, having come from somewhere specific. They will close the door behind them, radiating a feeling inside to the audience. Maybe they are scared, exhausted, or excited.

The player will speak, giving context for their behavior.
> If they're scared, huff and puff and yell, *I can't deal with these zombies anymore.*
> If they're exhausted, *That's the last time I work a double at Uno's.*
> If they're happy, *Shh! They could be here for their surprise party any minute.*

Then have them cross somewhere else in the room and ping off their environment.
> If they were being chased by zombies, grab a chair and barricade the door.
> If they are exhausted, unbutton your pants and slip on some sweats.
> If they're prepping for a surprise party, blow up a balloon and set out chips and dip.

Direct them to sit in the chair. Maybe it's to catch their breath, to cry to themself, or to check their phone. Then all at once, there's an emotional shift; they jump up and head back outside.
> Maybe they hear a zombie and arm themself with a kitchen knife before running out.
> Maybe they left the car running in the driveway because they were so tired.
> Maybe they see headlights in the driveway and go hide in another part of the house.

Once the track work is laid, another player will enter mimicking everything they saw. Followed by another and another just like in Cooey Cooey Cooey. Repeat and italicize every offer. Match the spirit in the eyes, tone, attitude, behavior and spine.

There is a tendency for people to only focus on the fun or funny parts. Note this they need to pattern all parts of the roller coaster. If it's just the highs and lows or peaks and val-leys, it'll feel disjointed. They should push themselves to hit all the blocking, all the lines, all the intentionality and emotional texture. Nurture the sentiment, make it matter, be truly terrified of the zombies, or worked to the bone, or geeked for your bestie's birthday.

Now cue the entrances at a quicker clip, so that players overlap with one another, one opening the door, another blowing up a balloon, another seated tracking their Uber, or bringing out chips while another runs off to hide. Eventually, let two enter at once, then three. Help them feed off each other and ratchet the emotion to a fractal kaleidoscopic end.

This illustrates the power of walking in other people's shoes, living and owning their choices, finding humor through simple truths, and making something extraordinary by investing in and celebrating the ordinary.

DOLPHIN TRAINING

When training an animal, the trainer builds a bond by creating language using operant conditioning. This is a principle found by B.F. Skinner rewarding a behavior with praise or food to encourage more of that behavior to happen in the future. Bridging is vital. When a curious dolphin interacts with a target, the moment the desired behavior happens the trainer must immediately acknowledge the behavior with the ding of a bell. This is the bridge, and that bridge is strengthened with some fish or squid. Eventually, the dolphin comes to realize that the bell means they are doing something right, and the reward of squid tells them they're doing great, and lots of squid tells them they nailed it. This positive reinforcement promotes curiosity, conditions behavior and allows the trainer to command a string of behaviors to execute bigger tasks with more complexity.

Improvisers don't want fish; they want laughter, they want applause, they want to be understood, they want attention and to feel connected. These rewards can be used to bridge and bond with your scene partners.

The Unsaid Note: Don't punish the dolphin. Don't scold it with words or show frustration. Instead have players focus on what is working. Reward the good. This keeps the scene alive, encourages more curiosity in the scene partner and emboldens in them an eagerness to try.

When an initiator scolds for not reading their mind, this leveled judgment makes their partner less brave, less adventurous, and less declarative. Players stop making choices because they don't want to make the wrong choice.

Encourage players to engage with their surroundings, to nose around, to make discoveries. That is how teammates breed behavior, expand their language and grow their bond. Trust can't be bullied, it needs to be nurtured.

Next, have a volunteer stand out in the hallway with their fingers in their ears. Those inside the room are given an assignment: Without words, using only laughter, applause, and eye contact for positive reinforcement, the *Trainers* must get the person outside the room, the *Dolphin*, to stand in the center of the room and sing their national anthem.

Trainers are often way too sparing with their encouragement. No one wants to reward obvious things like walking into the room. So the Trainers bite their tongue. Their silence feeds the Dolphin's anxiety. It makes the Dolphin cower and freeze at first and then become spastic, wildly jumping around the space desperate, uncomfortable and full of fear. The Dolphin acts like they are doing something wrong because the Trainers treat them like that. Without a bond, they feel insecure, timid, and self-conscious.

The Trainers need to throw the Dolphin a small fish here and there. They need to let the Dolphin know when they enter the room that they are seen, appreciated, and loved. In the grand scheme of the universe, the fact that the Dolphin entered the same room where they were supposed to sing is an amazing accomplishment. It deserves a reward.

Don't hoard your infinite stash of invisible squid. Use them!

An acknowledgment will make the Dolphin feel accepted. This endorsement validates their instincts and breeds more conviction, purpose and curiosity.

Just because players stand side by side on stage doesn't mean they are on the same page. There are infinite realities in improvisers' heads, infinite possibilities and directions to take a scene. When someone heads north toward your infinity — that's incredible. Reward that step. Nod, smile, hold them with your eyes. Let your scene partner know they are not lost, they're heading in a shared direction. This encouragement keeps them moving North. This adjustment changes everything. The judgment is gone. The playfulness abounds. Choices are rallied around. A weightlessness lifts the room, and the Dolphin will move with confidence where they must be and sing what must be sung. Players must find what they love in their scene partners, not what needs to be fixed.

Applaud the good instead of silently judging the bad. Bridge, bond and cradle the Dolphin's moves. This guides them through the dark. Give them sound, reward them with it, so that when there is silence they know it's for a reason.

No one would boo and hiss at a baby's first steps, no matter how graceless or klutzy. Applaud those steps, and rejoice in them to embolden the baby to take more steps.

This adjustment from stern dictator perfectionist to nurturing altruistic cheerleader opens and unlocks the team's psyche. Players sense the shift and Dolphins intuit exactly what they are supposed to do and soon enough are singing at the center of the room.

When trust is there and the bond is working, it's like a cheat code. Players are alert and without words, they cradle and lift the scene together effortlessly.

As the bond grows, challenge the ensemble with a scenic agenda for the Dolphin.

Example: The Dolphin enters the room, greets everyone, gets them to hop into a pool, then turns on a boom box to lead the room of elderly people in an aquacising routine to *YMCA* by the Village People.

Players can talk in character but may only chum the water. They cannot call out the shark. If the Dolphin enters the room and someone in the scene immediately says, *Oh, the aquacising teacher is here. I hope they play YMCA today during the geriatrics aquacising class.* This *calls out the shark.* So there is no joy in discovering the scene.

Instead, players can start by living in the environment— some may be swimming in the pool, others stretching on the side or putting on bathing caps— this gives context clues and helps the Dolphin get their bearings.

When they enter, players greet them with eye contact that demonstrates a reverence for them as a teacher. This *chums the water.* The Dolphin will see this information and interact with the environment and in a few moves they'll find their role, intuit where they fit because of how the players are treating them.

The Dolphin's job is to take a quick read of the room and try things. They may whistle yelling, *Everyone out of the water!* If no one responds, the Dolphin might flip it, *Everybody in the water.* And this move would be met with wild enthusiasm, fortifying their choice. A common trap is that players fear that making any sound will signal to their partner that they are 100% correct. This isn't true. Note it right away. Explain that there is a range of enthusiasm from normalcy to absolute exuberance. It's like a metal detector. To know the machine is working players need to hear it beep every so often, or they'll question if it's on.

For the Dolphin to feel acknowledged, they need to hear a base reality of beeps and boops. They need welcoming eyes, warmth, and enthusiasm to know they exist at all.

This exercise trains players not to make too many offers at once. This can cloud a scene and make it muddy. By playing a piece at a time, the Dolphin doesn't need to sort through and decipher what's getting the love. Keep it simple. Worry about where they are, who they are, then what they're doing. Use inch-by-inch victories to build confidence and support to complete the scene agenda.

Over time, challenge the ensemble with more sophisticated agendas.

Example: The Dolphin receives a briefcase, and then uses its contents to assemble a rifle. They then take cover behind someone selling helium balloons where they will wait for an odious czar to come to a balcony overlooking the square to address his people. During the czar's speech, when the clock strikes noon, the Dolphin will draw their gun and assassinate him.

In this example, the stage should be steeped in tyranny and oppression. The ensemble acts as the dregs of society, the forgotten, the angry underbelly as they spit on the street and glare with their eyes at the czar's balcony.

It's all about creating a stage picture and existing in the theatricality. This allows the Dolphin to drop into their surroundings and use that information to make an educated guess of what is needed. Nine times out of ten the Dolphin will spit as well and everyone will cheer and wink at them knowingly. The Dolphin will feel the narrative rise in them, that something must be done, and if they are listening they will find how they fit into the story.

DYNAMIC DUEL

Begin with two players in the center of a circle facing each other. Invite a player to offer an action with an emotion, then invite the other to respond with their own action and emotion.

Example:

> Player A waves hello to Player B and smiles.
> Player B rolls their eyes at Player A and returns to their phone with a sigh.

Don't let Player A be deterred and drop their deal. Urge them to stick to their choice and wave and smile again earnestly, trying to get their scene partner's attention. Player B shouldn't relent either; encourage them to keep snubbing their partner, by obsessing over their phone.

Players must commit to their initial instincts, cosign their first move, and trust that loving their idea will give it legs. Scenes wobble in the first few moves when players are deterred or defer to each other. Players are so accommodating that they sacrifice characterization for agreement. This wishy-washy politeness leads to characters without points of view and scenes without direction.

The first interaction in a scene is everything.

If one player barks as an assertive drill sergeant, and the other cowers saluting nervously, honor that dynamic and the DNA that is there. The more the drill sergeant barks, the more the private will flinch and shudder. If instead the drill sergeant suddenly swallows their bark, it dulls their choice. If the private suddenly stomps their foot and grits their teeth, it flips the script. Audiences need repetition to see the set behavior. Sudden, inexplicable, unearned shifts confuse the audience and send the scene spiraling. Drill this until players demonstrate an unwavering loyalty to their first choice.

As these interactions heighten, characters will naturally gravitate toward each other or away from each other. Note this push or pull. If they step toward each other have them get closer and closer with every move. If they step back, press them to retreat further. This uses proximity and stage picture to reinforce the interaction to make it more playful. Sometimes players will step closer but then stop once they are a *polite improvisers distance apart*. This stunts the growth and playfulness of the scene. Invite them to find infinity in these push and pull dynamics.

If a player ever retreats into a corner, surround them with the thing that repels them. This is classic slapstick. If Abbot and Costello are scared by a spider, they'll back away from it only to be trapped in its web. If a player takes a hors d'oeuvre from a caterer's tray and the caterer pulls back, then the player will help themself to another and the caterer will retreat further and further until they back into the circle. This activates the players in the circle to grab hors d'oeuvres as well, strengthening the interaction with sheer numbers.

DAGGER & HAIR

Begin with everyone in a large circle. Hold an invisible dagger by its blade and throw it across the circle to another player who will clap the blade between their hands to catch it. Players must throw the dagger crisply with intention in their eyes, hands, and entire being. As it cuts across the room, those not catching it should stay engaged *OOH*-ing as they trace the dagger through the air.

Some players want to be funny and have it stab them or jab in a wall, which is fine when drilling object work, but in this case, the focus is on intention and anticipation. The illusion of speed is created not by how hard the dagger is thrown but by how quickly it is caught. Readiness is everything. Players must be eager to field any offer. This level of awareness and engagement can be exhausting but endorsing each other is essential.

Playing correctly players start to see the blade as it moves ninja-like from person to person. This sets the base foundation for the exercise. It is the duck, duck, duck of Duck Duck Goose.

Next, introduce *the goose*. When a player receives a knife they have the option to throw the knife or to pull a long hair from their mouth. When they pull the hair, dread washes over their face, as they realize it goes much further than expected. The ensemble rallies to their rescue tugging the knotted clog of hair from the pit of the player's stomach. It is the player's job to writhe, framing the pain. Invite everyone else to recoil and play up the grotesqueness like something out of a Korean horror film. Eventually, the hair is yanked out with a nightmarish gasp, then everyone resets as the saved player throws the knife again.

The dagger and the hair both establish a causal relationship where X yields Y. Dagger thrown yields dagger caught. Hair on tongue yields a Cronenburg tug of war.

Next, introduce other options:
> Someone uses their phone to snap a picture and says, ***Everyone get in!***
> Everyone else swarms in posing like tourists yelling, ***Cheese!***
>
> Someone holds a conductor's baton and taps it against a pulpit, ***Ding Ding Ding.***
> Everyone else forms a choir belting out a single note, ***Ahhhh.***

Next, invite them to create their own, where X yields a group response of Y. Whatever response to X comes first, becomes the rule moving forward.

Example:
Someone enters holding a cheesecake saying, ***I bought cheesecake for everyone.*** If the first person responds ***Yay!*** Then everybody will match that yay with enthusiasm. If the first person barks, ***I told you I'm on a diet!*** then everyone adopts that growling frustration.

This blitz of causal relationships hones players' recall, commitment, and comedic/contextual reflexes. As they fold in more options to their repertoire, prompt players to enunciate responses with more detail and intensity. Challenge the ensemble to never show the audience the same thing the same way twice. It should always be improving upon itself even in the smallest of ways. Every revisit should be sharper, more real, more textured, more emotional.

Playing at a quick clip, there's no time to deliberate their choices and judge themselves. It's all instinct and celebration. This invites spontaneity and surprise into the work. The only thing anyone can control is how identifiable and distinctive they make their choices, so it will yield an identifiable and distinctive response.

Next, invite players to hybrid two prompts together to cue a braided response.

Example:

>Someone taps their phone against a pulpit. *Ding Ding Ding! Everyone get in!* Everyone swarms in like tourists belting out, *CHEESE!!*

These mash-ups help players hone their ability to repurpose games for third beats and rewarding callbacks.

RIVERWALK

Eight players plant themselves on stage. One is invited to move while the others remain stationary. The Mover serpentines the room, between fellow players. Once moving they cannot stop unless a stationary player begins moving. In that instant, the previous mover freezes, relinquishing the focus and transferring it to the new mover.

When players are moving their heart rate climbs, their vision narrows, periphery fogs, and even their ears drop out. Call it out. Moving creates blindspots. To try to take the focus in these moments, when the mover may not have their eyes on you, is chancy. It brings risk into the exercise. If someone is a clumsy spaz, their movement creates unwanted interference. When an ensemble risks too much too soon or is too undisciplined it sinks the exercise. Allow the ensemble to discover these dangers on their own and when it falters explain why it went wonky.

Emphasize the difference between risk and perceived risk. It's never about catching your scene partner off guard. It's about supporting them. If a player wants to move, they need to let the ensemble know they are moving: be bold, make a noise, and signal to them. The more agile the ensemble gets with this give and take, the more they can refine it until they are so nanoscopic that it appears they are reading each other's minds in soft focus, all impulse and anticipation.

Remind the players to breathe, stay calm and be open to the room, to all sounds. They should be a narwhal's tusk, sensitive to any action and change so that they are not closed off to the support of their teammates. Ensembles use restraint and conviction to create fluidity. They must communicate to move and flow as a single line of cursive. Challenge them to hand off the energy telepathically.

More times than not, this exercise becomes democratic, and overly fair. Each mover takes equal turns moving around the space for the same eight to ten counts before someone else takes over. Fairness is not funny, it's a funeral march lulling the audience to sleep. Call out the need for variety. No one goes to a concert to watch a metronome tick back and forth center stage. The audience wants modulation, two counts, twenty-eight counts, five counts, fourteen counts.

Push them to move like a river. Build to a point where the energy is unpredictable, the support is almost too quick. There will be mistakes. Sometimes two people have the same impulse and step out at the same time, then they freeze out of politeness as they ho and hum deferring to one another. When they hold the rules above their own instincts, they choke out the human element of the art form along with any surprises. This frames the moment all wrong, hemorrhaging energy and flow, and inadvertently drawing more attention to their misstep and cementing it as a mistake. It's a beautiful thing that they were so in sync, that they both had the same read of the room and the need for new movement. Don't let them telegraph panic to the audience. Instead, invite them to immediately match the steps and actions of their twin. Encourage them to move and mirror and orbit each other and find a way to crash their energy around one stationary person, transferring the focus back to a single entity. This way it appears intentional and there is no cause for concern. It was simply the way the river flowed for a moment before the water found itself again.

Help yourself and your teammates by following your foot. When it falters, when there are turbulence, rapids and hiccups, find ways to meet it with confidence and continued connection to show with certainty that it is just a bend in the river.

DRILLS

RANTING & RAVING

Begin with everyone milling around the space. Invite whoever loves babies to cross to the right side of the room. Next, everyone who hates cockroaches to the left. Anyone who loves holidays to the middle of the room and anyone who hates taxes to touch a wall. This builds a correlation with players. Opinions give them direction.

Next, ask everyone to jump in the air if they like dessert. Have whoever jumps the highest stay up, and ask everyone else to sit where they are.

Invite the player to rave and embellish about desserts. The raving energy is full of glowing enthusiasm that heightens to heavenly delirium.

It is not enough for the player to say, *I love candy*.

If they do, ask why. If their answer is *Candy's great.* Ask more questions, to conduct the scene. Help them use all five senses to share their love. Demand specifics, and make them make you believe they love the pucker and punch of a Sour Patch Kid. Applaud players when they use truth and details from their actual life to prove their point.

Remind the players not to be trapped by their own perceived ceiling. To help, instruct the ensemble members on the floor to gesture with open hands as though they are ushering a cloud up into the sky. This acts as a visual cue for the raving player to keep growing and heightening their love.

Players rarely permit themselves to obsess this way. Underline the inherent power in unpacking their character's opinions with specifics, justification and tenacity.

Next invite two players up, one on the right side of the room and the other on the left. Interview them both for things they love and hate.

One loves Birthdays and another hates Bedbugs. Now have them flip it. The player who loves Birthdays will rant about how much they despise them, and the player who hates bedbugs will rave and adore them.

This can be challenging for players. They need help divorcing themselves from their characters. Just because players' feelings don't align with their characters doesn't mean they can't tap into the wealth of knowledge and experience they have on the topic. A player's love can be flipped to fuel their hate. Hate the pucker and punch of a Sour Patch Kid. Despise the army of gummies attacking your pancreas by the handful.

To help players unpack the bitter hostility of their rant, instruct the ensemble members on the floor to point and prod with accusing fingers damning the player to the pits of hell.

The instructor will conduct both ranting and raving monologues gesturing for players to speak and heighten their point of view. Remind players to start low on the Richter scale so that there is room to grow the scene and earn the redline emotion. Even though players are unpacking their own topic, they must work together to ratchet the energy between them.

Begin with a player lovingly raving about bedbugs and as that grows from a 5-6, handover to a birthday rant seething from a 6-7, then back to the glory of returning home to a house crawling with adoring bedbugs at a 7-8, then quicken the pace. Encourage players to *time-dash* and *turbo-jump* to up the ante and make these obsessions and points of view playable, switching back and forth between players until it hits a pinnacle ten.

Don't theoretically discuss what happens when a Mento is dropped into a Coke — show it. Hold the Mento over the two-liter bottle and drop it in. Place characters close to the things that drive them mad or make them swoon.

Example:

> RANTER: *Oh whoopee, my sister's here with some stupid little gift to remind me I'm another year closer to the grave!!*

> RAVER: *Who's hungry?! Daddy's home!! I missed you all so much!!*

> RANTER: *I'm trying to eat a meal. Do I really want you knocking on my door and having to get on a sweater and a bra because you feel like singing Happy Birthday? I'm not a baby!!*

> RAVER: *Hi, my babies! Did you miss me, your blood-flavored Capri Sun juice box of a man?*

Next, invite two players to share a rant and two to share a rave in this same fashion. Here players cosign and finish each other's sentences. Think: *Beastie Boys* rapping directly at the camera replacing one another mid-rhyme but continuing the line of logic with shared energy. Insist they stay invested, cheering and championing each other. No player should be standing, waiting as a spectator, thinking and crafting their own ideas while ignoring their partner. Stay engaged, otherwise, too many ideas will fracture the focus and fun.

KEEP THE ...

Begin with five players. Invite one to declare themselves an object as they contort to become it on stage.

> JALEN: *I am a witch's cauldron.*

Eva enters as an object and places herself in relation to the first offer.

> EVA: *I am a bubbling brew in the cauldron.*

It is important that each addition to the stage picture chain link to a previous offer.

> DAVY: *I am the eternal purple flames forever burning under the cauldron.*

This creates relationship, context and dimension.

> FINN: *I am the witch's broom stirring the bubbling brew.*
> NORA: *I am an ancient etching of a rose on the staff of the broom.*

Challenge the ensemble to endorse each other's moves to create a single vision, paint with the same brush, and share the artist's eye. All moves should cohere and connect to create a portrait, not a page out of a child's activity book where tractors and apples float out of context and scale.

To that end, when a player declares themselves *a mildewy backpack*, all moves should invest in that choice. Everything should be caked in mildew, grime and mud. This aligns players' choices with their teammates. It walks in their footsteps to build scenic cohesion, a line of logic that the audience can plug into and enjoy. This is an essential skill for world-building.

> WALLACE: *I'm a mildewy backpack.*
> NELLI: *I'm a chewed pencil missing its eraser.*
> MARKIE: *I'm a notebook.*

Here a descriptor was lost, Markie sacrificed specificity for speed — Call it out. Stop the drill and allow the player to revise their offer.

> MARKIE: *I'm a ratty notebook with a coffee stain.*

Drive home the importance of texture. When descriptors are ignored, they become recessive. Neutrality breeds neutrality, swallowing scenes and worlds.

Once the ensemble is proficient at building these portraits brick at a time, add to the exercise.

> JALEN: *I am a witch's cauldron black as tar.*
> EVA: *I am a hissing hexed potion brewing in the cauldron.*
> DAVY: *I am an eternal purple flame forever burning under the cauldron.*
> FINN: *I am the witch's broomstick, cut from a cursed tree, stirring the bubbling brew.*
> NORA: *I am an ancient etching of a rose branded in the staff of the broom.*

With all players positioned in this witchy tableau, explain that anyone within the group can yell, *Keep The Blank!* And that object will stay and all others will vanish to the backline. Now it is the ensemble's job to re-contextualize the object, for example, the Etched Rose, in a new picture with its own aesthetic.

> NORA: *I'm the etching of a rose.*
> FINN: *I'm a beefy biker girl's bicep raring and ready for her rose tattoo.*
> DAVY: *I'm a rusty tattoo gun rattling and spurting blood and black ink.*

Once all five players are positioned in the tattoo picture, a player will yell to keep one of those objects and the ensemble will re-contextualize it.

After a few portraits, invite players to add detail and find ways to be more theatrical and intentional with their choices. If a choice is made as pointillism, continue to draw with that same technique. If something is done as a watercolor continue with watercolors. If a statement is declared with flowery Shakespearean language, double down on it. Breathe life into your portraits with the timbre of your voice and the gravitas of your language. Listen to the picture to accentuate its DNA.

Now, have the players return to the witch's cottage. Have them say all the specifics they said before but this time with more bite and cackle, and state every offer with maniacal, nefarious delight. Then, at the seedy tattoo parlor embrace the toughness and when the tattoo gun is sputtering ink and blood have everyone make the noise, make it so loud that the others have to shout to be heard over its rattle. Challenge the players to make these images pop to draw the audience into their imagination.

Next, challenge the group to create an analogous picture that can be transposed directly on top of the previous picture, where the subjects relate to one another in the same ways. It may help to reference the famous image of six marines planting an American flag after the Battle of Iwo Jima and the image of New York City firefighters pulling a flag pole from the wreckage of the World Trade Center.

Initial Portrait:

JALEN: *I am a witch's cauldron black as tar.*

EVA: *I am a hissing hexed potion brewing in the cauldron.*

DAVY: *I am an eternal purple flame forever burning under the cauldron.*

FINN: *I am the witch's broom cut from a cursed tree stirring the bubbling brew.*

NORA: *I am an ancient etching of a rose branded in the staff of the broom.*

Analogous Portrait:

JALEN: *I am a French chef's immaculate all-clad stainless steel gourmet pot.*

EVA: *I am a simmering bone broth with lemon wedges and apple cider vinegar.*

DAVY: *I am the blue flame of a pro-grade Viking range, dependable and exact.*

FINN: *I am a large hand-crafted sterling silver acorn soup ladle by Johan Rohde.*

NORA: *I am an acorn insignia engraved on the hand-crafted ladle*

Improv: The Art Of Collaboration

This demands that each player understand their role and how they function in the picture. The cauldron's function is to hold a hexed potion. As the first player, Jalen can make any first move, an aquarium tank, or a baptismal fountain, so long as it serves the same purpose of containing something.

Function is crucial to establishing a successful analogous beat. No matter how much a player's character or environment changes, if their function and relationship to each other stays the same it will allow for scene partners to effortlessly plug into the new dynamic.

SIDESHOW

Platform the exercise by commanding the class's attention, channel P.T. Barnum electrifying the crowd with bravado.

> INSTRUCTOR: *Come one. Come all! Get your seats, squeeze in close. I am Silas B. Goddrey and boy do we have a show for you tonight. From the straits of Gibraltar to the mountains of dark Peru I've scouted some of the most incredible talents living on this blue marble we call Earth. Tonight prepare to feast your eyes on a parade of freaks, weirdos, misfits and genuine geniuses.*

Gesture for applause.

> INSTRUCTOR: *First up, we have something truly unnerving: Minerva the girl with a spider face and a penchant for simple gymnastics. Let's hear it for Minerva!!*

Then gesture to one of the students to take the stage as Minerva.

If there is enough enthusiasm in the room a student will hop up and take the gift, using their hands as mandibles, showing off their spidery face before doing a simple cartwheel or somersault. Cheer and underline how amazing it was that the player took the invitation without a second thought. Stress how important it is to pump up the crowd and be clear with offers. Don't make your scene partner work to decipher your gifts. Place them square on a tee so teammates can knock it out of the park.

NEWER PLAYERS MAY NEED A TEMPLATE: *Up next we have INTERESTING NAME with a INTERESTING PHYSICAL DESCRIPTOR and an uncanny talent for INTERESTING ACTIVITY.*

Once introduced, each player will enter stage right, show off their talent center stage, bow to uproarious applause, and then introduce the next act before exiting stage left.

> PLAYER A: *Up next we have Kyle Sinclair, the ten-month-old baby who's the fastest shot in the West.*

Kyle immediately takes the gift and enters crawling to a stool center stage. There, gurgling and wide-eyed, they find a gun and bullets and show off a series of trick shots before taking a bow and introducing the next act.

This drill is all about clarity and commitment. The longer players delay, the more they overthink offers, the more precious and self-conscious they become, and the less likely they are to wow the crowd. The worst thing for a player to do is shrink in the face of a gift. Take it on immediately.

The same is true in scene work, if someone declares you the nerdy teacher's pet, show it instantly. Adjust your spine. Be affected by gifts. Show the audience that you are fearless, poised, and ready to pounce on any offer, no matter how stupid, to make it magical.

Building off this exercise, have everyone form a circle. One player hops in the center. A player from the outside gifts the player inside with an attribute and occupation, OCD Gardener.

The player inside spins on one foot and lands, transformed, bent down singing to a tulip with a spade in her hand. *LA-LA-LA!* They count out each *LA* on their hand to make sure they say exactly three, this makes the attribute instantly playable. The player monologues in character, heightening and exploring their gifts. *Each tulip gets the same attention. No more. No less.*

Next, the players on the perimeter strike poses becoming objects enwreathed around the character. Some may be tools, fertilizer, bottled water and seeds, shovels, or rabbits. These offers surround the player as points of stimuli to inspire them. Think of a rock being thrown in a still pond. The rock is the gift. It makes a splash, and that gift ripples out to create more points of inspiration.

Next, build to full-length scenes. Begin the same way by gifting a player with an attribute and occupation, A Sickly Basketball Player. The player spins on one foot and lands in a chair on the sideline of a basketball game wheezing and asthmatic.

> PJ: *Go Barons! Do a swish! That's how it's done!*

Other teammates inhabit the environment. Player B paces the sideline as a disgruntled coach. Player C is a medical alert necklace on PJ's neck. Player D is a water cooler at the end of the bench. Player E, Lacy, sits next to PJ riding the bench.

> LACY: *Will you shut up, Chauncey! Why are you so into this game?*

PJ points at Player B and contextualizes them.

> PJ: *Cuz Coach says if I keep the stats good all year he'll put me in. We have a gentleman's agreement.*
> LACY: *That ain't never happening.*
> PJ: *Yuh-huh, he's gonna let me loose on that court, so I can show'em what mom's little miracle can do.*

PJ gestures to what was supposed to be a necklace and declares it as his jersey.

> PJ: *I even wore a jersey just in case. See?*

LACY: *103?*

PJ: *Yep, just like 103.1 the Christian Rock Station.*

LACY: *How do you get this excited when you're not even playing?*

PJ: *Just because someone's color blind doesn't mean they can't enjoy a rainbow. I can! It's just all purples and grays. Fortunately, gray ... my favorite color.*

Lacy crosses to Player D and pours himself something from the cooler.

PJ: *Can I ask you a personal question, what's it like to drink Gatorade? I can't because my heart's too big for my body.*

TAKE-OFF SCENES

Begin with four players shoulder to shoulder in a sprinter's position. When the instructor says go, the players race across the room. The first to reach the other side begins an action, such as sweeping the floor, and the other racers immediately assimilate the action, sweeping in kind.

Next, one of the four establishes, non-verbally, how they feel about what they are doing. One may sniffle a sad whimper and immediately that sentiment is adopted as their collective *OOH*. Regarding *OOH*, it is imperative to echo it back. If it goes unacknowledged or sneaks by unmatched, this emotionally charged dominant offer becomes recessive and fades into the background, swallowed by neutrality. Don't let players get so lost looking for a scene that they forget to listen to it. When you hear an offer, bold it, underline it. Let it know it was heard by repeating it and giving it the attention it needs to grow.

Now the four will continue the action while committing to the emotion. The more they sweep and clean, the more they will weep and cry. Push them to be earnest and believable as opposed to broad and cartoonish.

Encourage them to feed off each other. When they feel they are all in agreement and on the same wavelength, one of them will say *Yep* and then all four will clap at exactly the same time signifying that this scene is done. They will run out of that scene, touch the other wall and then run back across the room to do a new scene with a new action and emotion, such as making smoothies happily.

Improv: The Art Of Collaboration

These take-off scenes are designed to capture the mad dash adrenaline rush of taking the stage to platform a scene. The length of the room acts as a runway for the players to build momentum. They run into a scene with togetherness, committing full force without even knowing what the scene will be. They fearlessly jump and let the net appear. This is the spirit of an ensemble. This is having someone's back.

I've got your back doesn't have caveats. It's not, *I've got your back, as long as I understand your idea.* No. Players need to run into danger together. That is how they build trust with each other. They commit, support and endorse whether they like the idea or not, whether they understand the idea or not.

Imagine soldiers storming Normandy with that caveat in their heads. The boat hits the shore, the ramp lowers and a single soldier runs down to the beach and the others watch waiting to see if their idea works. It would have been an even bigger blood bath than it was. Players need to storm the beach together. Jump on grenades for each other. What matters most is that they hit the stage and commit to each other. There is no going back to the starting line; they are committed. Momentum pushes them past fear, panic, mental blocks and self-preservation.

When players are on the backline they'll lean against the wall or on their own heels. This is a physical brake, a safety measure. Humans are wired to avoid failure and pain, but improv needs failure. Players need to be willing to make mistakes and fail spectacularly. Lessons need to outsmart our wiring, by putting our bodies in front of our brains. That is why the exercise begins in a sprint. It makes a game and race out of it. When someone races across the room and makes a declaration the others glom onto it without question because they are already invested, and committed, and there is no time for hesitation.

Some players have a hard time adopting an idea they don't understand. They don't want to be wrong so they stand studying their scene partner instead of playing along. Note it — Invite them to match the physical choices. Help them see that when they stare at their scene partners trying to solve the scene, they stand out for the wrong reasons.

Clarify that the initiator is not responsible for steering the scene. Once the action is defined it becomes public domain as a shared activity. If the first person extends their arm up in the air and the others do as well, someone else may *YES, AND* that and unscrew a lightbulb and carefully replace it with another, which would lead to everyone unscrewing lightbulbs and replacing them. However, that same initial action could be

YES, AND-ed so that they were all picking apples in an orchard. If the action is undefined and open-ended, don't stand there petting Schrodinger's cat in your mind; take action, make it a light bulb or an apple or some freak show where people eat light bulbs like apples. When players commit to an action for more than eight counts and nothing is growing, more likely than not no one knows what they are doing. Empower anyone to make a choice and share it with the group in the name of clarity. Scenes should always be in a state of being or becoming. As they progress they should get more specific, detailed and nuanced. If it starts broad and stays broad, it is everything and nothing.

Everyone has their own energy, sense of humor, and point of view but when they leave the starting line they must get on the same wavelength and find the scene and ride that wave together. Having the players yell, *Yep* and clap at the same time is a galvanizer. It acts like a clap board syncing all sound and motion and sentiment. Over time, invite them to substitute the clap for some other synchronized moment that naturally occurs in the scene if they are all gargling mouthwash perhaps they can all spit in the sink at the same time.

Sometimes players rush the *Yep*. This comes from a lack of connectivity or a misunderstanding that speed is the aim of the exercise. It is not. The aim is to create playful and actionable scenes with confidence and connectivity.

Some permutations of players will have too much connectivity and not enough confidence or vice versa. Call out these anemias. Some players get a quick look at the start and then disappear into their own little universe for the rest of the scene. They may not even hear other's offers or the *Yep*. Insist on two parts eye contact to every one part object work. This keeps everyone connected and feeding off each other. Even in fishing scenes, the target should never be the improv fish. The target is always your scene partner. Whenever there is meaningful eye contact you are hitting the bullseye, whether you catch fish or not. Don't Gollum-out with your precious object work — stay connected, share what you have, and don't hoard the ring. Otherwise, you get tunnel vision and disappear from society, and the next time you look up years have gone by and you are a self-obsessed troll divorced from society. Stay connected. Don't be seduced by your own clever imagination.

With more reps, players start to embrace emotion and assimilate action effortlessly. Scenes become dynamic and playful through simplicity. Although the exercise is intended to have quick take-off scenes, the scenes stretch longer and longer. The players forget the assignment and get lost in the connectivity. To feel so seen and so heard is exhilarating. Tapping into a state of flow, all time melts away as they bask in their connection.

Next, allow language but only to add specificity, texture and dimension. Words should never shortcut the action or the emotion. Phrases like, *I am very sad* or *I like shoveling* are unnecessary. These should be shown, not said. Help players understand this or take away language until they do understand it.

Next, combine the Spotlight exercise with the Take Off Scenes.

Example: Four players begin trying on jewelry and giggling.

Here not everyone needs to be matching each other at all times. One player can be the interesting while the others are interested. This mechanic allows the exercise to become more scenic and lets the players conduct the scene from within.

One player tries on an emerald ring, posing and showing it off, while others gasp in delight.

Then another becomes Interesting trying on a ruby-encrusted bracelet and the others can Ooh, gasp and giggle at them. Each offer must get the attention and interest it deserves. Don't let these scenes get *And-happy*, or they'll become a boring list of jewelry without any emotion.

Reactions give traction to our scenes.

When players understand its power and value, they will be more apt to invest in the OOH. If the OOH feels flat and fake, it cheapens the scene. We need to believe in our make-believe. Make things matter by caring and crying and pouting and cheering. Emotion gives weight, stakes, depth and realism to our worlds. Case in point, I went to my niece's gymnastics meet. When her name was called over the speaker, my sister stopped talking mid-sentence and her eyes focused on her daughter as she entered. *She's doing the balance beam.* My sister yelled to her. *You got this! I believe in you!*

I should mention that my niece was three years old and there was no balance beam. Instead, it was ten feet of bright blue painter's tape stuck to the dark blue mats with a hula hoop on either side. My niece jumped into the center of a hula hoop and then began her routine, walking across the blue piece of tape.

This could not have been less impressive. There were no stakes. No danger. But my sister leaned forward, her eyes fixed on her daughter; with each step my sister was drawn in more and more. When my niece got to the other end of the tape, she hopped into the other hula hoop, and my sister jumped out of her seat and cheered. And I jumped out of my seat and cheered. Because it mattered so much to my sister, it mattered to me.

This is the power of OOH.

My sister's investment and enthusiasm elevated a piece of tape into a high-wire act.

Think of the tape as the trajectory of our improv scene and my niece as a character moving along that narrative line of logic. Each step and move, each *AND* is met with *OOH*, rejoicing in the moves elevating the stakes, the fun, breathing drama and importance and life into the scene.

Players often obsess about outdoing every *AND*; instead players should outdo their celebration of every *AND*, each *OOH* bigger and more earnest than the last. Our *OOH* allows us to share with the audience how we feel about every move we make: how it affects us; how it changes us; how it feeds and fuels the scene. If instead my niece had come out and just walked across the tape and hopped in a hula hoop in complete silence, there'd be no spectacle. The fanfare elevates the ordinary to something extraordinary. When we don't *OOH* or have any opinions about the scene we're creating, it will feel as flat and safe and boring as a piece of tape on a padded mat.

THE BACKLINE

New players think the backline is a place where they're safe and invisible. They roll their eyes in their heads, muttering opening lines under their breath, rocking and tottering with doubt, itching in their impatience, or taking a sip of their beer. The backline spotlights all neuroses and insecurities. It should never upstage the scene. Help players recognize when they steal focus for the wrong reasons. Have them calm their breathing to collect themselves.

Comedy is Tragedy plus timing, so acting on impulse is everything. If a player has an idea on the backline but they're sluggish, by the time they rock forward and follow their instincts the audience has already predicted their move and it lands stale. Help players stay a step ahead by being loose and ready. This starts with their stance.

A young cornerback's speed can be their ruin. They know they're fast so they wait, sit on their heels and assess the QB, the routes, then race to break up the pass. Eventually, the passing gets quicker, the QB reads progressions faster, and the corner's legs can't cover the field. A good coach calls it out early before it becomes a habit. *You're flat-footed! You on vacation? Start the snap on your toes. You're better than this!* The slight adjustment of rocking forward, leaning into the present moment, on your toes, anticipatory, fills players with potential energy. There is less lag between instinct and action. They gain a step and buy back the time they'd been losing because their mind and body are ready to plant and cut as one.

The same is true for the backline; players lean back on the wall watching a scene, and they might even lock their knee and heel as a brake in front of them. It is their ego protecting them from making dumb choices. When that player has an idea, they rock forward tripping over their own locked leg, a literal ego trip. In this stutter, they miss the window of opportunity and then rock back to the backline. Call it out before it becomes a habit. *He who hesitates is lost.* This posture puts the self before the team.

Backline work can be drilled just like scene work. Make it a game, begin with a player on stage holding a wand. As they summon items, the backline will rush to make the magic materialize.

Examples: A Pinball Machine, A Moped, The Seattle Space Needle, etc.

This trains an ensemble to work together in a split second to create stage pictures that cohere. Taking this drill into scene work helps players realize that their hands are their wands. When they gesture to their futon covered in Beanie Babies, it is an opportunity for the backline to swarm in and support.

As another drill, assign a common keyword to the backline before the scene, such as, *Because*, *Only*, or *Sometimes*, etc. Anytime this word is said the backline rushes out to become their environment, or scene paint, or simply drop and do three push-ups. This sharpens a team's agility and alertness.

The backline's eyes should be fixed on the scene, fixed on the Interesting. Cradle the scenic energy, hawklike and attentive. If a teammate goes on a tag run building momentum and hilariousness, be a fan of their moves. Fixate on the funny. Your eyes are a laser pointer directing the audience's attention on where to look, and what to appreciate.

If players glaze over deep in their own thoughts and pre-planning, call it out. Quiz the backline after pieces. Ask them to highlight other teammates' moves they loved in the piece. If they hem and haw, it's a sign that they were busy designing what's next rather than engaging in what was right then and there.

New players sometimes hide like wallflowers on the backline. Call players by name. When they hear their name, they need to initiate and anyone else can enter to support the scene. When the scene is over the instructor will call scene, then call another name. Some scenes may only be three lines long, and some players initiate three or four scenes in a row. This keeps everybody present in the *Now* where there is no time to plan.

The readiness is all.

The audience is a passenger on a 747 that is our show. When there is turbulence, they white knuckle. When the flight crew scrambles in a panic, they hyperventilate. Don't give the audience cause for concern. We want to entertain them and make them laugh, not worry or fear for us or fill them with a sense of doom.The audience must trust that the performers are professionals, that the show is going to take them on a journey, and that they are in capable, confident hands, or the performers will not hold their attention. When initiating, love your idea, and enter with swagger and commitment that draws others into your orbit, and your world.

While I was growing up, there was always an army of relatives over whenever anybody had a birthday. One year, we were singing happy birthday to my sister in the garage, when mid-song, we heard an engine rumbling down the street blaring music and everyone stopped singing and turned to check out the car, a black and gold Trans Am Firebird. It was my Uncle Mark. He looked like one of the Ramones. He was the only adult I knew with long hair, a beard and an earring. He was lanky six foot three. He jumped out of his car and held up a plastic tub of bean dip.

UNCLE MARK: *I got the dip!!*

And people cheered, matching his energy. Some relatives actually walked over to him and he grabbed a plastic spoon and started slopping bean dip onto everybody's styrofoam plates. People lined up for it because he was so excited about the gift he brought. He was unapologetically in love with his idea and it made people who had already eaten and were ready for dessert want to have a little of his idea on their plate. This is *Uncle Mark* energy.

On the other side, my cousin worked at a grocery store and one year she brought a kid named Howie to our Christmas party. We have a very loud clichéd stereotypical Italian family, so everyone was nosy.

AUNT DONNA: *You two dating?*
AUNT NAN: *Is she dating him?*
AUNT LINDA: *How do they know each other?*
AUNT DONNA: *Any wedding bells?*

Howie was dead quiet, barely made eye contact, and never took off his ski jacket.

The next year, my aunts approached my cousin and gave her the third degree.

AUNT DONNA: *Where is he? Where's little Howie?*
AUNT NAN: *You two break up?*
AUNT LINDA: *He wasn't right for you.*
AUNT DONNA: *No, not him — good riddance.*

Then my cousin pointed.

COUSIN: *He's right there.*

He was standing in the corner with a wet bag of unopened potato chips. He'd been there for half an hour but no one noticed him. He didn't love his own idea enough to even offer it. He was invisible, quietly haunting the house with *Howie Energy* instead of owning it.

When we're on stage, play with Uncle Mark energy. Lean into your choices with your whole self. Be devoted to your gifts, undeniable and unflappable. If you don't love your scene ideas, you can't expect your teammates to love them either.

When a player's confidence in their scene begins to erode, when Howie Energy creeps in, they'll slowly inch away from the audience toward the backline where they feel safe. This literal retreat is a tell. Most players are unaware that their body is betraying them. They're so inside their own head and disconnected from the stage that when they are edited they're shocked to be on the backline. If a player can feel themself retreating, invite them to move upstage with confidence, grab something with intention and cross downstage to anchor with authority.

If they feel themself shrinking or their scene deteriorating, invite them to reconnect with their scene partner, re-invest in what has been established, and react to what is happening in the now to right the scene and regain the trust of the audience.

SCENIC EXERCISES

TOUCH TO TALK

Begin with two players up. Give them a suggestion of a relationship between two people, such as a pharmacist and a customer. They will start a scene with the directive that they must touch to speak.

Done poorly this is painful to watch, an empty gimmick, where players touch not out of motivation, but desperation to talk. Silence terrifies them. Words are their armor. When they aren't speaking they feel vulnerable and weak and exposed.

This touch-to-talk rule reveals so much. If players are observant and honest, they'll admit how little they move on stage, how little they embrace theatricality and how uncomfortable they are when asked to move with meaning or be anything more than a talking head.

Explain how this simple rule demands they commit to live in their bodies and their choices. They cannot move without earning it. They cannot touch without reason. This helps them use words sparingly. It charges the stage picture with proximity as they play with heat and weight. It rewards physicality with information. It builds a direct association so that when players feel lost on stage, all they need to do is connect. Whether they are touching or not, they realize every moment has its own gravity and importance.

Work with the silences. Use the space and moments between lines to bring weight and tension. Invite players to feel what their characters feel. Let their silence speak and use it to add depth to their scenes.

Another approach uses touch to intensify. Players must think of themselves as having a built-in turbo button. Whenever their scene partner touches them, it activates them to intensify their emotional state. If they are sad they become extremely melancholy. Touch them again, they will shake inconsolably. Again, they will move to wallowing exhaustion.

Sometimes players begin a scene holding their cards too close to their chest, so close no one can clock their emotions or identify their sense of self. This technique creates a clear interrelation where touch becomes a catalyst. The character levels up, still the same soul and spirit only more pronounced. This allows a player to conduct their scene partner, literally pushing their buttons, to show their cards and grow their game.

PEAS IN A POD

Two players sit side by side as they are interviewed Christopher Guest style about a vacation or event they attended. As peas in a pod, the goal is to heighten and explore, finding ways to share sentiment while building a narrative. Don't let them just sit there waiting for their turn to speak, urge them to be active listeners, engaged, nodding in total agreement with their partner, eager to finish each other's sentences.

As a cheat, players slow things down, filling their scenes with air, and searching for what to say. Call it out. Have them speak at a normal clip. If they're still stalling, they're likely stuck in their heads inventing. It is hard to create in a void. Invite them to share real world specifics from an actual trip they took. If they are still stumped ask them questions: Was it a long drive? Was there good food? What was the best part? What was the biggest letdown?

Every event people attend is a roller coaster. It has its ups and downs and corkscrews and loops and long waits and exhilaration. Questions help the players visualize the ride they experienced together. As they answer and make declarations it gives their shared past a shape.

The players are positioned shoulder to shoulder just like on a rollercoaster, so that they are aligned with each other, facing the same direction, taking every bend and turn and loop together.

When they have agreement and fluidity, give them a thumbs up to indicate that they can pivot from past tense to present tense. Suddenly they are poolside having fresh melon and French toast sticks. They snap for the waiter to top off their mimosas. This past to present shift is vital to making sure players are playing their games not just relaying their games.

Peas in a pod scenes are about endorsement, having someone in your corner to champion your every move. These exercises begin centering around a big event but can grow to non-eventful tasks like folding clothes or ordering Grubhub etc. When players endorse each other in the right ways, they can find the ride and fun in anything.

HYPE MAN

Two players begin side by side. Player A shares an honest statement, park bench of truth style. Player B, the hype man, makes their partner 110% correct. They can embellish whatever was said and cite examples of past behavior to prove Player A right. They want to fan the flames of their partner, building the scene from an ember of truth to a hot flame to a burning inferno.

> PLAYER A: *I worry sometimes I'm not enough.*
> HYPE MAN: *That's an understatement. When Josh-y got accepted to college, he called the school to double check they didn't make a mistake.*
> PLAYER A: *My whole life I guess I just felt kind of invisible.*
> HYPE MAN: *Sometimes he is. Like those automated doors at the grocery store, they never open for him. He's like practically a vampire.*

When players fortify simple statements it creates instant propulsion. Within four lines Player A has become a figurative vampire. Now, encourage the players to take the figurative and make it literal and actionable. The Hype Man may cross downstage and open the shade to let light in and watch as Josh hisses in pain, recoiling at the sun.

SLOW BURN SCENES

Begin with four players off-stage. Suggest a location, such as Starbucks. A player enters making three statements that evidence their opinion about the environment.

Andrei retrieves a drink, examining the cup.

> ANDREI: *This says Arvid but my name's Martin. Is this mine? Hello? Whatever.*

He rolls his eyes and grabs the sugar shaker.

> ANDREI: *Excuse me, the sugar's all stuck together!*

He shakes his head in disappointment. When he pours the creamer, it glops out of the container rancid and sour.

ANDREI: *This place sucks.*

Every step, statement and opinion sings the same story. This sends a clear signal to their scene partners.

If instead Andrei questioned the coffee but loved the oat milk, then was sad that they didn't have any more cake pops, these zig-zags makes it impossible for the backline to track any pattern or line of logic.

Player B, Leah, enters underlining what has been established through repetition.

She examine her cup in the same way.

LEAH: *This says DiDomenico but I'm Doug. Is this supposed to be mine? Hello?*

She shrugs, roll her eyes and grabs the sugar.

LEAH: *And the sugar's all stuck together here!*

She shakes her head in disappointment then sniffs the creamer, and winces at the sour smell.

LEAH: *This place sucks.*

At any one of these moments, Player A can turn to Player B and say,

ANDREI: *I was just saying the same thing.*

This is their Austen-ian thunderclap moment when two strangers cross paths who see the world the same exact way. It is kismet and sparks instant synergy. The two players commiserate with each other, then make a new discovery that forwards the scene and backs up their opinion.

LEAH: *Look they blocked the outlets, so we can't even work here anymore.*
ANDREI: *It's like they don't even want us here.*

Once they've unpacked this discovery, Player C enters with an emotional *OOH* that aligns with the established game. This gives their entrance oomph and makes it that much more impactful.

Sophie groans, furious.

> SOPHIE: *That's it!! I'm done with this place!*

Sophie gestures holding a tiny cup in their hand, shaking their head, irate.

> SOPHIE: *This is their new venti!*

This sends the three players into fits. Lastly, the fourth player enters with another game move to spike the energy, heightening to riotous discontent.

Sometimes players drop their energy to field an entrance. Note this right away. When playing a slow burn scene, it's a given that all four players will share the same sentiment. This removes any guesswork. Every entrance and offer, even if it's gibberish, is an instant catalyst, permitting players to become bigger versions of themselves.

PASS THE PHRASE

Begin with four players in a circle. Give them a starting phrase of anything at all. One player will re-state that phrase to the player to their right, and that player will repeat what they heard and how they heard it to the player to their right. As the phrase passes counterclockwise, the phrase will be reduced to gibberish.

It's important to note that players are passing what they hear, not what they know it to be. This takes some work because players' brains want to make things make sense. Encourage players to let go and allow the phrase to devolve. It needs to cede to chaos before it can be wrangled into something new.

Example: *Stack The Chairs.*
> JULIA: *Stack the chairs.*
> OWEN: *Stat the chairs.*
> MIA: *Statsdachairs.*
> TESSA: *Statsdachairs.*
> JULIA: *Datsdachairs.*
> OWEN: *Datstashares.*
> MIA: *Dats ta shares …*

The moment a player hears that it sounds like something new, they grab the phrase and step into the circle, signaling to the others that they're wedging the scene open to make it actionable. Mia repeats, **Dats ta shares ...** Then *YES, AND*s it, *... **I brought hummus and pita chips for us ta shares.***

Instantly, the three other players will match the tone, speech, and spirit of the player initiating. **Dats to shares** becomes their chorus to repeat as birds of a feather.

> TESSA: ***I brought glasses and fizzy water for us to shares.***
> JULIA: ***For us? No. This is yours.***
> TESSA: ***No. Dats to shares.***

Often players will clean up the grammar, valuing clarity over character, such as ***That is for us to share.*** Note this right away. Don't let players strip the texture from the phrase. It severs all characterization and makes it dull and toneless. The gibberish slathers the phrase in mustard. Invite them to relish in its relish. Whenever players can trick their brains, bodies, or tongues into making new choices, invite them to embrace it, and let it surprise them.

When this scene reaches its height, have the players grab a new line sharply from the scene and pass it in a circle to their right until it devolves into gibberish. As an emergent phrase arises use it to wedge and platform another scene.

Sometimes players let all the consonants drop away which leaves them with a shapeless Gregorian chant of vowels. Note it — They don't want to file the texture of these words down or there'll be nothing to grab.

This exercise rewards brave bold players. No one can think or plan ahead because opportunities are only open for a moment before they morph into something else. Encourage players to grab for the golden ring on the carousel because the next time it comes around it may not be there.

Once this exercise has been platformed, split the room into small groups of three and four and allow everyone to get reps at the same time. Emphasize the importance of letting go so that phrases can become non sensical, then plucking an idea and punching through the chaos like saloon doors to establish a matching scene.

Next, challenge four players to do three scenes in a row, passing the last phrase from each scene until it inspires a new scene. At the height of the third scene, have the players pivot to characters from the first or second scene for a callback.

Players can be timid and precious about grabbing the focus. They often wait for a *perfect* initiating line to emerge. This results in a hypnotic eddying whirlpool that sucks all energy and confidence out of the room.

If something sounds a little bit like something, it's enough.

The last thing players want is to have the audience hear initiations before they are stated, or worse hear initiations that are missed altogether. Fortune favors the bold. Grab the chaos before it's recognizable to stay out in front of the audience's expectations.

Players may hold the reins too tight by correcting language or even ignoring offers so they feel comfortable. Help them let go. Stress that scenes must go wild so that they can be wrangled, and then set free, so they can go wild again. If players always have control, they will never develop a skill for lassoing/taming the chaos. Without that skill, they will only feel comfortable clinging to their same choices, characters and relationships. Improv needs chaos, danger, and discoveries. Otherwise, it's just a rerun of successful scenes from the past.

TWO-HEADED MONSTER SCENES

Begin with six players up. Two will be designated as the *two-headed monster* and the other four as backline support.

The instructor whispers to the two-headed monster an attitude about their environment that they both will share: *This airline is divine.*

The two players platform the scene establishing their opinion and environment with emotion and object work. In this case, they take their seats, and remark on the luxurious fabric, the ample legroom and the lavender-infused air.

GABI: *Oh, the seats are so pillowy.*

STEVE: *And there's so much legroom. I don't want to get up.*
GABI: *This airline is divine.*
STEVE: *It's heaven.*

These declarations signal a very clear message to the backline, activating those players to support the scene in kind.

A flight attendant enters from the backline with pillows stuffed with baby goose feathers.

Any offer made by the backline is meant to feed the beast. It is permission for the two-headed monster to grow their attitude. They are the emotional barometer of the scene, and every offer is another log to burn their fire brighter, bigger and hotter.

The backline players must give them space to process, react and unpack each gift before piling on too many logs. Let them exhaust the fun before overwhelming them with another offer. Restraint is easier said than done. Note it when it's not there — Each offer must be made with patience and an ear for rhythm to make sure that the flame isn't snuffed out by the offers. Players get excited when they know the game. They want to get in on the fun with their bacon-wrapped scallops and foot massages. Just because they have an idea doesn't mean it's time for the idea. Wait for the violists to finish playing take-off music, let the two-headed monster make a meal of that, and then when it's time, serve your idea at the right moment to build the scene into a blazing bonfire.

> ## *Be a better waiter. Listen to the rhythm of the scene and to the laughter to find the right time to deliver your offer.*

Players must identify if the two-headed monster is extraordinarily impressed or if the plane is extraordinarily impressive.

The above example runs with the idea that the airline is extraordinarily impressive and subsequent moves fortify that choice, making it a heavenly decadent experience. However the scene could be replayed with the same sentiment, only this time an ordinary airline would be perceived as extraordinary. So instead a flight attendant passes nonchalantly and says, *Please make sure your seatbelts are fastened.* And the two-headed monster is touched by the flight attendant's concern.

GABI: *They're so thoughtful!*
STEVE: *More than my parents ever were.*

This frames a normal plane as spectacular and sets a rule for the backline to gift accordingly with common airplane offers that will be met with insane enthusiasm.

This exercise scaffolds the keys to great support work, clarity, patience, timing, emotionality, and framing with likeminded moves to surround characters with what tickles or tortures them.

We want to torture our characters.

This exercise progresses to the two-headed monster having differing attitudes about their environment. This demands more patience from the backline because each offer must be unpacked in two different ways.

The instructor whispers to the two-headed monster that they are both at a Harry Potter-themed restaurant. Trevor sees it as a tourist trap rip-off and Ines believes everything about it is absolutely magical.

The two players platform the scene establishing their opinions through conversation and object work. In this case, they take their seats.

INES: *Honey, I can't believe it! They sat us in the Gryffindor section.*
TREVOR: *Lindsey, please, this is how they get you.*
INES: *Personally, I think I'm more of a Hufflepuff but I'm not going to say anything.*
TREVOR: *They make you feel like a Gryffindor so you spend like a Gryffindor. It's a rip-off.*

These declarations should activate the backline. They can either embrace the ordinary nature of a theme restaurant or celebrate the magic, where a waiter appears out of thin air with a round of butterbeer. Ines will clap with glee while Trevor rolls his eyes at the price.

THE AUDITION

Begin with four players seated facing the stage. Explain that their characters are producing a film together which they wrote. Today is the first day of auditions. They are classic Hollywood narcissists obsessed with their script and in love with themselves. Instead of playing them mean and biting, ask them to shower each other with compliments. It should sound like an echo chamber of *Yes-Men* bragging and smug.

Let them run and riff with these prompts. Push them to finish each other's sentences and literally pat each other on the back to establish who and how they are. As the scene swells, the instructor will cue their first actor to enter the audition room. Before the performer can even speak, the panel will gush about how perfect they are for the part. Any compliment that is given by a member of the panel will be trumpeted by the others. They circle and bold each offer with absolute agreement.

As this reaches its height, a producer gestures to the actor and says, **Whenever you're ready.** The panel flocks back to their seat and settles. The anticipation is palpable. All focus shifts to the actor who takes a breath. The panel leans in on bated breath.

The actor scrambles in out of breath. They run back to the door barricading it immediately.

> *Junior prom, my uncle's cabin, it'll be fun!*

The actor crosses downstage center. They open a cupboard and grab canned corn, they open it and shove it in their mouth, then cough and begin to cry.

> *Why did I have to be the only one to get away?*

The actor nods and says, *Scene.*

Without a second, the producers erupt from their seats raving about the performance. They take turns recounting the smallest choices, praising their delivery, the dialogue. Every compliment is echoed by the others. As the energy peaks, one of the producers will place their hand over their heart and say, *There was just one thing ... If I may?*

All focus shifts to the producer who takes a breath. The panel flocks back to their seats all ears.

The producer performs the very brief scene emboldening all the original choices either with dramatic tension or with melodrama, then they can say, *Scene.*

Again, the producers rave about the performance until another holds their hand over their heart and says, ***There was just one thing ... If I may?*** This pattern continues as each producer takes their moment to heighten or butcher the original performance. No matter how good or bad the reinterpretation, it is always met with reverence until it crescendoes into a self-congratulating song of praise.

FACTS & FICTION

There are few things worse than unabashed commitment lopped off at the head. Imagine a player flaps onto stage, swooping in as a menacing dragon. They circle the players and then land with a roar, belching hellfire from the pit of their stomach. They're so convincing that the audience can see the dragon's colossal tail snaking its prey. They lower their chin, drop their winged arms and ... all physicality and character goes with it. The entire illusion is lost. They're revealed for what they are: a lazy improv nerd perched on a cafe chair.

Don't sell out your choices. When kids dress up for Halloween they transform. They give over to the costume and attitude. They channel the character.

As we grow up we're more self-conscious. When we don't know what to say, we feel more judged, watched, or looked at, and that makes us half-commit to the fun. Don't let players stand on stage holding a cheap plastic mask of their idea.

A common defense for most players is, ***I don't know what else a dragon would do. Seriously, what am I supposed to talk about?***

When players are tentative to take on high-concept gifts, invite them to tap into what they do know. Huge high-concept ideas need grounding. Marry the extraordinary with the ordinary, the mundane with the magical.

Even if it doesn't jive with pre-existing tropes associated with their character, the juxtaposition is unexpected and allows players to tap into real human behaviors instead of inventing Tolkien-esque nonsense. Begin by asking everyone to think of a factoid, something they find fascinating. Like when polar bears hunt they cover their black nose with their paw to blend with the snow. Or how to perfectly poach an egg in an air fryer. Invite them to unpack why it's fascinating for them and their character. This grounds the fantastical with actual knowledge.

Next, two players will create a scene. Before they begin ask Player A to think of a factoid and hold it in their head.

Factoid: Native to the Bolivian and Peruvian Andes, the potato first arrived in Germany in 1630. According to legend, King Frederick II of Prussia believed in the economic and nutritious value of potatoes. But the countrymen wanted nothing to do with them. King Frederick even tried to make it a law demanding all farmers plant the so-called apple of the earth. But they all refused. So he decreed the potato a royal crop, one to be guarded night and day by soldiers. However, he commanded the guards to look the other way at night. Soon peasants and people from all over the country would sneak and steal potatoes planting them in their fields and in a few short years it was their main crop. Highly valued foods taste even better.

Now Player A will be gifted as an imaginary creature. Player B's job is to play along with the narrative, follow the fun and call out the weird stuff when it happens.

Example: A kid, Veronika, has just moved to a brand new school in rural Minnesota. It's winter, cold and lonely. The kid begins building their first snowman and as they put the hat on its head they wish for a best friend and with a little magic the snowman, Player A, comes to life.

The fun is playing with these tropes. The narrative is already loaded and saccharine. Nudge Player A to commit to the physicality of moving like a snowman. Have both build the scene and when it's time to rest that dynamic, cue the factoid, challenging the snowman to weave it into the narrative.

> VERONIKA: *I can't believe you're real!! You're really real.*
> SNOWMAN: *Be-lieve it! Just like King Frederick II of Prussia believed in the economic and nutritious wonders of the potato.*
> VERONIKA: *I guess? Anyways, I'm just happy you're here to be my friend.*
> SNOWMAN: *Whoa, you can't force someone to be your friend, just like King Frederick II couldn't force the countrymen of Germany to eat potatoes.*

VERONIKA: *Are you just going to keep talking about potatoes?*

SNOWMAN: *The so-called Apple of the Earth? Don't mind if I do.*

VERONIKA: *Please can we talk about something else, like where are you from?*

SNOWMAN: *Oh me? My home's in the Andes Mountains between Bolivia and Peru.*

VERONIKA: *Wow! All the way from South America.*

SNOWMAN: *Yep, just like the potato.*

VERONIKA: *Okay. I think my mom's calling now.*

SNOWMAN: *You're not going to fool me with that little lie the way King Frederick fooled an entire country into planting, eating, and harvesting his delicious potatoes.*

IMMOVABLE UNSTOPPABLE

The words immovable and unstoppable conjure a stalemate, an impossible war. In sketch, this dynamic is choreographed and rehearsed with tactics, strategies and emotional shifts. It is a break-neck ride and it's possible because it's written. Every turn and drop of the rollercoaster is planned.

In improv, this type of scene needs absolute agreement. Players must shed their egos and find ways to fail in their scenes. It's an agreed tug-of-war between partners. That's the dance they do for the audience, giving and taking. One steps forward and the other steps back. It's a hydraulic. One wins so the other can fail. This creates peaks and valleys, drama and tension.

It's one thing for players to intellectually understand the need for failure, it's another to allow themselves to lose. Newer players usually don't have the guts to have their characters fail in an improv scene. The fun is in failing. Nobody leaves an improv show and says, *Oh that was so nice how nobody looked foolish.* They want to see people fall and get stung by bees. No one wants to see Wile E. Coyote catch the Road Runner. They want to see him fail at it. Improv 101 should never be about looking cool and being in control. Improv is a lesson in failure and humility. How can we be okay with failing in public? Players can't take what happens to their characters personally. They must release their ego and lose for the scene to win. It's a hard concept to accept. Players' brains are wired to win. They want to prove what they know, how witty and smart they are. This is why failure needs to be baked into an improv curriculum from the very start.

This exercise requires an awareness of scene dynamics for players to discern when it's time to shift the scales in their character's favor or to their dismay to advance the scene.

Begin with two players on stage. Assign one the role of Immovable Object, and their objective is to stay in the scene. The other becomes the Unstoppable Force, and their aim is to get the Immovable Object to leave the scene. Bringing these diametrically opposed viewpoints to improv can be challenging. Stress the importance of players working together to fight, just like stage combat.

Now gift the players with a relationship that plugs into this dynamic: A Parent, the Immovable Object, has just moved their Child, the Unstoppable Force, into their college dorm room.

The parent begins anchoring themselves to the scene.

> MOM: *This is so exciting, isn't it, college life? Isn't it cool?*
> CHILD: *I guess. But don't you need to get going?*

Remind players their characters are related. They have a history and love for each other. Don't let them just kick their parent out to win the scene. They need to earn it.

> MOM: *Could you imagine? What if we were roommates?*
> CHILD: *Mom! Don't lay on her bed. What if she comes in?*

At the moment, the parent is winning. The child should embrace their role and find ways to whine, be embarrassed and pout and lose more.

> MOM: *Ooh, I know, let's hang up your posters. Where's that sticky tack we bought?*
> CHILD: *No! No! C'mon, Mom. I'll do it later.*

This *NO* acts as another line in the sand. Players can say *No*, but encourage them to play along with the action.

> MOM: *Okay, you're right, first things first, let's unpack and organize all your clothes.*
> CHILD: *No, Mom. C'mon, I don't need you to do that.*

The players should make a meal out of everything. The Mom arranges the drawers just so, while their Child sloppily dumps everything in one drawer.

> MOM: *C'mon, that's not how I raised you.*
> CHILD: *Mom, it's fine. It doesn't need to be perfect.*
> MOM: *Wait, what are we thinking? I bought you those fancy hangers that smell nice.*
> CHILD: *I don't need those.*
> MOM: *You said you did. You begged me for them in Bed Bath and Beyond. Which bin did we pack them in? I'll have to go through all of them.*
> CHILD: *Mom, you're seriously going to go through all of these?*

The Mom has won long enough. It's time to shift the scales.

> MOM: *Oh my, it's hot in here. I'm wringing wet. Want me to go buy us some waters?*
> CHILD: *No, Mom, I'm fine. I can get my own water.*
> MOM: *Nonsense, I think I saw a Dasani machine down the hall. Dasani's on me. I'll even get one for your roommate.*

When Mom leaves, the room is quiet. The Child is winning. They take a breath and flop down on their bed, giddy. They text on their phone and then smile. They look around their room and for the first time, they feel independent. They glow with self-satisfaction. Then the door flings open and Mom enters struggling with something.

> MOM: *Look, someone was throwing out this perfectly good fan.*
> CHILD: *Mom, people are going to think I'm some weird dumpster diver.*
> MOM: *I don't care, It's a sauna in here. Drink your water.*
> CHILD: *I'll have it later.*
> MOM: *It'll be room temp later.*
> CHILD: *Mom, I love you but you have to go.*

Mom sits in silence.

> CHILD: *Mom, did you hear me?*
> MOM: *Yeah. I know.*

Mom stands and hugs her Child and swallows.

> MOM: *You're right. You're right. I guess, I just ... don't wanna leave.*
> CHILD: *I know.*

Improv: The Art Of Collaboration

This can be an understated schmaltzy moment. The Mom embraces losing, laying it on so thick that the Child actually wants her to stay.

> CHILD: *I guess you can live here with me.*
> MOM: *No.*
> CHILD: *We'd just have to keep it a secret.*
> MOM: *I mean, you know I would, but I can't.*
> CHILD: *You'd just have to be very quiet all the time.*
> MOM: *No thanks, it's too hot. Plus I gotta hit the road.*
> (Looks at watch) *It's already eight.*
> CHILD: *Mom, you won't be home until three in the morning.*
> MOM: *That's okay.*

They are now fighting to lose. It's a form of improv jiu-jitsu where the player uses their scene partner's force against them.

> CHILD: *No, are you sure? I'm worried.*
> MOM: *Don't be worried.* (Yawns) *I'll be fine.*

The movie, *What About Bob?* is a textbook example of this. Psychiatrist Dr. Leo Marvin (Unstoppable Force) assigns his patient Bob Wiley (Immovable Object) to take a vacation from his problems. Bob takes the assignment literally and uninvited joins the Marvins on their family vacation to Lake Winnipesaukee. This dynamic could easily go stale. But the film doesn't. The characters are rich, full of emotional weight, tactics, and antics and the stakes keep ratcheting higher, to the point of inversion, delusion and then euphoria.

WHERE DID WE COME FROM?

Begin with two players on stage. For their suggestion give an event or location. Have them exit, then enter the scene having just come from that place carrying objects and opinions with them. Use their immediate past to heighten and explore their current mood and relationship.

Humans don't just materialize out of a puff of smoke. Characters are like tumbleweeds

—where they were shapes who they are and informs how they feel now. Let them stomp in with the slosh and stink of sewer water soaked through their shoes or ride high on the momentum of having just won fifty bucks on a scratcher.

For characters to feel real, they need history, a past that grounds them. They existed before the suggestion. They woke up somewhere and took a bus or bike to get to the scene. This builds a world beyond the stage. They have homes, jobs, plants to water, bills to pay, and promises to keep. Their apartment was just fumigated, or they pigged out on free samples at Costco and need GasX again like last time.

Even using the words *Again* and *Last time* has this same grounding effect. It turns a one-time occurrence into patterned behavior. It plants in the audience's mind that this character has always been like this.

As an outside assignment, have players take note of how people actually enter a room. They'll observe that everyone wants to tell you where they just came from, the hellish or heavenly day they had, how slow the train was, how bad the service was at Sweet Green, or how they ate a pizza burger that gave them diarrhea.

Don't let players waste their entrances and exits. Make them memorable. In a sitcom no one ever enters a scene unnoticed. They arrive with a Kramer-y jolt that changes the atmosphere of the room. They enter playing their game: geeked out, depressed, humili-ated, sneezing or sick.

When characters have a past, that history is a gift. It provides richness to their scenes. When characters arrive with something in their arms, it's an artifact to be treasured. Even if it's micro-mini cupcakes, obsess over them.

> ANNE: *Look what we got! Micro-Mini Cupcakes.*
> JIM: *Aren't they the cutest?*

Don't shut up about them.

> ANNE: *Honestly.*
> JIM: *Be honest!*
> ANNE: *Have you ever seen something so adorable?*
> JIM: *Ever? I don't even want to eat them!*

Hijack the book club. Go straight to the kitchen and look for the perfect platter.

> ANNE: *We want a big platter!*
> JIM: *To make the cupcakes look even smaller.*

If players enter as a two-headed monster sharing sentiment, it allows the scene to heighten and move faster narratively. However, if they have disparate energies, allow more time for each character's individual game to be played.

Example: Paige enters furious, with a huge orange foam finger, having just come from a Syracuse University basketball game.

> PAIGE: *Double overtime and they lay an egg with that choke job?!*

Claudia follows close behind unfazed and chipper.

> CLAUDIA: *Hey, they gave it their best.*
> PAIGE: *Well, Roy, their best isn't good enough!*
> CLAUDIA: *Ripping up the team calendar you bought won't change the score.*
> PAIGE: *That's it! You're right. I'm starting a fire. I'm going to burn this foam finger!*
> CLAUDIA: *Don't!*
> PAIGE: *And this beer koozie.*
> CLAUDIA: *Absolutely not.*
> PAIGE: *I'm done with them. I wish I never almost graduated from that school!*
> CLAUDIA: *I think maybe you should go and take a bath first and get that orange paint off before it ends up all over my couch. Plus I should look at that black eye of yours.*

OBJECTIFICATION

As a reference point for platforming this exercise, assign players to watch the *Merrie Melodies* short *Wackiki Wabbit* where two hungry castaways encounter Bugs Bunny on a tropical island. At the start, the castaways float on a raft lost at sea. They are so hungry they hallucinate and see each other as hamburgers and rotisserie chicken. This projection reduces their companion to a symbol of their wants.

Begin with everyone standing in a circle. Ask a volunteer to take center and declare themselves as an object, such as an iPhone. Invite the others to envision the player as an iPhone. In no order, the ensemble will direct statements at the player. These statements must be legitimate declarations someone could say to another person, and at the same time, they must be truthful statements about the object itself.

I can't live without you.

Sometimes I want to throw you out of my car and never look back.

I like sleeping with you next to me.

You're so behind in the times.

Maybe it's time I move on to something new.

I don't know how to turn you on anymore.

You make me seem so much smarter than I am.

You open me up to so many things I would never have experienced.

Underline how these statements are charged with importance. They are amazing first lines that get to the heart of things because they are statements rooted in relationships.

> I feel this way about you.
> This is how I perceive you.
> This is how you make me feel.

Now ask the player in the center to recall which statement was most impactful and made them want to respond straight away. Drill this skill by rotating every player to the center as a new object or symbol. Encourage players to speak in run-ons to invite more detailed initiations.

Example: Old Couch

I used to hide behind you when I was little.

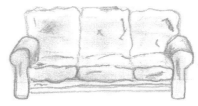

Whenever I was scared, I'd curl up in your arms.

You were always there for me.

You're stained. You're an embarrassment to this family. You hear me? You don't belong here anymore.

As the ensemble gets more comfortable with the exercise, have the player in the center cross to the initiation they liked best and begin a scene. The rest of the circle will immediately sit to watch.

Next whisper the same object to two players, Cheesecake. Allow them to visualize their scene partner as the object and use the same calculus to create a statement aimed at their scene partner.

> LENA: *I want you so bad right now but I really shouldn't. I can't cheat.*
> THEO: *You are a heart attack waiting to happen. I don't know why I like you so much.*

These opening lines pack a punch that truly honors and invokes the suggestion, instead of just shoe-horning cheesecake into the first line like a random Madlib. If players ever lose perspective have them visualize their scene partner again as that cheesecake from the same angle and the words will come.

What doesn't work is cycling through too many perspectives and angles on the same object.

> *You're a heart attack waiting to happen, and you're dried out. You're too rich. You're bad for me. I want you on my birthday. I can only take a little of you and then I feel nauseous.*

This is messy. Unless you're playing a character that's kind of all over the place, it's going to confuse the audience, and when they feel dumb they hate the players for making them feel dumb. Keep it simple; paraphrase the first statement.

> *I want you so bad but I know I shouldn't, I can't cheat. I keep cheating and it's wrong but I'm sitting at work this morning and all I could think about was having you for dessert all to myself when I got home.*

Holding on the one perspective keeps the character's point of view consistent and makes the audience feel smart for seeing the patterned behavior. Now that the scene is cemented, the player can blurt out the metaphor they've been holding as a prism in their head to give it language and shape.

> *I know this is gonna sound silly but you're like a cheesecake, I know you're bad for me, I'm only cheating myself by picking at you, hooking up in the middle of the day, getting motel rooms, but I'm lying to myself. This isn't the me I want to be. But I can't stop.*

This takes the metaphor and lifts it to a place of poetry. This type of statement needs to be earned; otherwise it'll overwhelm the scene and seem desperate to hit the suggestion. It's usually better for players to build behavior through repetition, and then reveal the metaphor to the audience in an elegant way.

ACTION & REACTION

Begin with a backline, and invite a single player to initiate with object work. A second player gets a quick read and joins with a strong response overflowing with details and context.

Example: Player A enters eyeballing a table downstage right. They inch stealthily towards it, dip their finger in a pie and lick it, savoring it. They sneak a pinch of bread, and a lick of frosting, delighting in the deliciousness.

Player B gets a read of the scene and, as the first to speak, enters with a sharp and scolding tone.

PLAYER B: *Prince Davies, this may be your birthday feast but you are not to steal away another bite. This is yet to be tested by the royal food taster. And considering what happened to your poor mother, and father, and uncle and grandfather and sisters and ...*

PLAYER A: *But I'm the birthday Prince.*

This exercise can be played as quick-fire two-line scenes or as longer more patient ones. Just because they are short scene starts doesn't mean they can't put a ton of detail and craft into them. Challenge the players to be the epitome of their ideas, exude behavior, radiate status and hold it in their spine. Even without words their ideas and offers should be playful, magnetic and undeniable.

The goal is to hone the ability to make a quick read and deliver a dynamic reaction that builds context, scene dimension and importance.

> *When a character draws a line in the sand, it means we've struck a nerve. Play and pluck that nerve like a violin string to create tension and stakes.*

Although Prince Davies is being scolded for his behavior, push him to continue to get his character into improv trouble. Say Yes with his eyes as his hands disobey, sneaking behind his back to take two fingers of tahini, a black olive, a sip from the gravy boat and some goose liver. The want for delectable delights outweighs his fear of poisoning.

Just because somebody shakes their finger at a wolf doesn't make the wolf any less hungry, any less desperate to eat the sheep. Characters must know their nature and stick to it. Don't let your characters be bullied into submission; it robs the fun and function from the scenes.

Don't just pour yourself improv lemonade and take a single sip, waiting for your scene partner to do all the work. Take a sip of Country Time pink lemonade, feel the sour in your molars and the condensation on your hands when you set it down, and question the aftertaste. *Why does it taste like baby powder?* Breathe life into your offers. Make them real. Exist in your choices.

Don't just Febreeze the couch. Febreeze it with disgust in your eyes. This will pose a question in the audience's mind; why are they disgusted? And it will awaken an answer in your teammates.

Don't just eat generic improv food, be specific. Eat Chef Boyardee Beefaroni straight from the family-size can while crying. Why are you crying? Because this is the first real meal you've had in weeks since the divorce.

Struggle and futz to get a lawn mower started in the hot August sun. If our struggle is real, a reality will unfurl from it. Player B will approach, gruff. Let their first line be a run-on. Let them hit like a wrecking ball.

> PLAYER B: *Are you kidding me? Are you serious right now? We're bringing my son, my six-year-old boy, out of a church in a coffin and you're out here during the whole Mass trying to start this stupid mower, wearing your Tampa Bay Buccaneers jersey, swearing your ass off!? What, this can't wait fifteen minutes until we have his tiny casket shoved into the hearse? You really need to cut the grass right now, right now! Does everything have to die today?!*

CHARACTER GAMES

A character's behavior can be so rich and real, it becomes its own game. *That's so them!!*

There's no one sure-fire way to create a character. Some pull from fact or fiction, others use status or chakras, physicality or emotion. Whether they are built from the inside out or the outside in, all characters need behavioral integrity and consistency. The performer channels the character so that every reaction, declaration, offer and discovery resonates and rings true to the character game.

When establishing patterned behavior in scene work, think of the audience as a giant baby playing peek-a-boo. The first time you put your hands together over your face, then remove them quickly to reveal your eyes yelling peek-a-boo, the baby doesn't laugh. Everything is new to them, so everything has equal weight. This offer is just a single star in the cosmos.

But if it's worth doing once, it's worth doing three times. Do it again: hands together over your face, then reveal your eyes peek-a-boo. This time there's a glimmer of recognition in their face. They are starting to put a little hypothesis together — Hands reveal eyes.

Do it again and they burst into laughter and delight in their prediction coming true. They laugh because they know it is going to happen. They feel like a genius, able to predict the future. Most of a baby's life is a wash of information, non-stop stimuli and randomness. So this is a powerful feeling.

And just like peek-a-boo, players have to teach the audience how to see and rejoice in our patterns. Keep them simple: when this happens, this follows. It is important to repeat our behaviors multiple times in the first minute of our scenes so the audience can recognize the patterns and put together their own hypothesis.

Over time the baby and audience tire of a simple flat pattern. Players will ditch these choices out of desperation to keep the audience's attention. Don't bail on the pattern or discard behavior; instead give it greater sophistication by heightening emotion, specificity and stakes. Find ways to revolutionize the character game.

That's when we put our hands in front of our eyes but we drop them to reveal our eyes instead of parting them. The baby howls in delight. This reinvigorates the fun, by giving the audience exactly what they were expecting in a brand new way.

Improv: The Art Of Collaboration

CHARACTERIZATION - INSIDE OUT

Characters should have a soul, a spirit, a temper, a tenor, a song they sing or principles they fight for, tricks they keep up their sleeve or secrets they hide in their heart.

These scene exercises build from the inside out. Delve into your character's wants, mine them for detail and comedy. Find the thing that drives them, follow it head first, ask what type of person sings this song, marches to this drum, and obsesses over these petty details. The answers to these questions give spine and shape to our essence, turning the flicker of a soul into a fully actualized character with quirks and idiosyncrasies.

WINNING & LOSING

Sometimes, the universe feels like it's stacked against our characters. Other times they're on cloud nine, invincible and everything's going their way. Any character falls somewhere on the scale of thriving to barely surviving, from a seven to a one. Pinpointing exactly where they stand on this character vs. universe pecking order is crucial. Knowing these numbers gives our characters consistency and behavioral integrity.

These numbers give player's brains something to chase. Rather than thinking of all the improv rules they're not supposed to break, they focus on their number and how they can continue to show their number through behavior to the audience.

Invite everyone to get a feel for these numbers by moving around the room and taking on these qualities as they're described. It's important they feel the weight, the unfairness, the struggle as well as the levity, mastery and bliss.

A One means the universe is stacked against a character. Every time they reach into their pocket they find a hole; when they open their lunch that got squashed in their backpack, it's gone rancid, the mayonnaise bad and their GoGurt exploded on their iPad and when they try to clean it, it slips out of their hands straight down a sewer grate. For a One, things go from bad to worse, quickly. They slouch, bite their lip and fidget and scratch, their neck turtling into their chest, trying to be as small and safe as possible.

As characters notch up the scale from Two to Three the universe isn't quite as cruel and unrelenting but still stacks against them.

As a Four the world is neither kind nor cruel. Playing neutral or indifferent can be boring and uninspiring for players. Invite characters with this number to find the fun in things being bitter/sweet. For every positive, there's a negative. An *Even Steven* character may win a new car but gets tons of parking tickets because of it. They may be drenched in the rain but they love rainbows so it's okay.

As characters climb higher from Five to Six the universe conspires in their favor. It's kinder, more giving, and abundant, luck goes their way, and green lights abound. Their shoulders square; their chin and chest out, they walk with purpose and swagger, poised, and persuasive.

At a Seven the universe anoints these characters as perfect, superhuman, gods. Even their mistakes are enviable.

Now that players have held those statuses in their spines, they can call those numbers back into their bones.

Next, the instructor demonstrates an occupation with an assigned number:

Personal Assistant - 2. The instructor bumbles with a phone. When they take a note the Post-its are stuck together or their pen won't work. When they try to fix it they get ink on their tongue. When they print something they're out of toner, and none of the keys seem to open the filing cabinet.

Each time a character interacts with their environment it's an opportunity to show that character's number. The character is a tuning fork pinging off everything they touch to sing their number and show the score between them and the universe.

Now, the instructor demonstrates the same occupation, touching the same items, with a new number:

Personal Assistant - 7. They answer the phone with ease, Post-its fly across the room like ninja stars and stick precisely where they want them. They pull files from the cabinet with authority. They are a master of their desk.

Improv: The Art Of Collaboration

Showing our number, our deal, is everything. Imagine a magician performing a card trick but rather than showing everyone the card keeping it to themself. If the audience isn't privy to the card, no one will applaud when it is revealed. The same is true for playing these numbers. Players can't be coy. Characters must show their cards to the audience. The universe may be on a character's side but it's the player's job to signal that fact to the audience. Be theatrical; instead of simply setting a pen in its holder, spin it, throw it into the air like a baton twirler and trace it with your eye as it sinks like a spear exactly where it belongs. Eyes telegraph what a player sees and they are also a window to how much a character struggles or how satisfied they are with themself. Bookend actions with approving or disapproving eyes to show your number to the audience.

Even a simple task can tell the audience a lot about who you are. If a character blows their nose in two quick bursts, then folds the tissue in half before tossing it over their shoulder into a waste basket, this telegraphs to the audience that the character is a five or higher. They are systematic, adept, and a good shot.

If a character blows their nose, then shows eyes that are panicked as they futz with their free hand searching for another tissue, then struggles to mop the snot off their face and winds up with a wet clump of tissues disintegrating in their hand, this communicates very clearly that the character is a two or lower. And when they try to shoot that clump of tissues into a waste basket it thuds to the floor, or worse hits a co-worker.

Play your number to show your number. Be crisp and deliberate.

Begin with two players up. One chooses a number, one through seven, in their head. They will receive a simple task such as making a sundae or pumping up the tires on their bike. They perform this task to show their cards, sharing their number with their scene partner through their interactions with their environment. The other performer is asked to watch and identify their scene partner's number. Instead of calling out the number, invite them to play along, as a hype man, gifting in kind through scene painting.

For example, using a One blowing their nose, the scene partner would get a read of their number and point out that they have snot on their lip, or Kleenex stuck to their face. When the player gets up to throw away the tissue, they'll point out that it looks like they sat on a chocolate bar. Their job is to spotlight their scene partner's number and fortify it with detail as well as pity or admiration.

Up until this point, characters have been playing their numbers through action and physicality and radiating emotion through their eyes. Now invite performers to use language to add detail and texture to the scenes. Be mindful that the same rules apply to language. If a character is a One, no matter if they use too many words or not enough, they will still never clearly express what they mean.

> **Too many words - 2:** *Hey you! You! Over there with the shirt, yeah you, here, hit me I'm open, pass me the bouncy basketball! Can you see me? Hello?! Oops, my bad. Cantaloupe? Yeah, thought it was a basketball.*

> **Not enough - 2:** *Hey, pass basketball!*

If the character is a Seven they may use many words or barely any at all but it is always well put.

> **Many words - 7:** *Whether you're a Blazer, a Buck, a Laker or a Hawk, you're nothing without a team. Run with each other, play for each other, don't force a shot, pass the basketball.*

> **Barely any words - 7:** (snaps) *Ball!*

Next, get everyone on stage. They will all exist in their own worlds. As they move around, assign everyone a profession and a status number: **Waiters - 6**, **Dog Walkers - 2**, **Ski Instructors - 7**. Encourage them to make discoveries. Status numbers can contradict job title or rank – players can be a Pea-Brained Captain, a Tongue-Tied Boss, or a Brilliant Busboy. Play with these inconsistencies. Be Weirdo Wedding Planners and Timid T-ball Coaches.

Audiences read people. In a millisecond they take in a character's posture, how they hold their heads, if they're froggy, regal or refined. Then they rank and categorize them into a social hierarchy: high or low, feared or revered.

Occupation, wealth, sex, age, race, background, achievements, knowledge, and ability — all of these character elements can overwhelm a player. Simplify it. Playing a character's number keeps the gameplay consistent.

Lastly, get two people up. Quietly whisper each a status number, and let both know the number their scene partner receives, so they can gift accordingly. Then give them a suggestion of a relationship. Throughout the scene, they should try to play their numbers in everything they do.

Afterward, the students watching will guess at each player's number and share rationales for their guesses. Watching in this way makes players more aware of each other's physicality and choices, and makes them that much more proficient at recognizing it in future scenes.

CUL DE SAC

Invite the ensemble to close their eyes to focus on a story. Ask players to picture they are at home. They hear a screeching sound. They run to their window and see the neighbor's car doing donuts in the cul-de-sac. Then the car careens out of control, hitting their mailbox. The car slams its brakes, parks in their neighbor's driveway and then they see the neighbor's ten-year-old run from the driver's seat to the house.

This story becomes a shared narrative for all characters. It is their collective *What?* At some point in this exercise, they will each be asked to recount this sequence of events through a character lens.

Next have players hop up and mill around the space. The instructor will offer a character prompt and the players will instantly take on new mannerisms to honor that personality, for example, Dean of Students.

Some deans might be stern, needling and ruthless, whereas others might be desperate to be approachable and cool. Encourage transformative choices to truly affect how players act, how they move, what motivates them, what words they use, and how critical or accommodating they are to each other.

As the Deans move around the space, the instructor will call a player out by name. Everyone else will sit. The character crosses center knocking on an improvised door downstage. The instructor answers playing the parent of the mischievous child. It's the player's responsibility to relay what their character witnessed out their window. However, it is even more important that their character lens influences how they tell their story.

When that scene is over, everyone jumps up taking on another character prompt: Bible Thumpers, Party Animals, New-Age-y Artists, Comic-Con Geeks, Flirty Town Gossips, Want-to-be Stand Ups, Obnoxious World Travelers, etc.

Performers are often so focused on platforming a premise they forget to embody their character to play the fun and the specifics of who and how they are. If they just rattle off: *Your kid was doing donuts with your car and they ruined my mailbox,* note it — they are snubbing the opportunity to explore their character. Plot points listed without personality leave the audience wanting more plot. Unpack these points with characterization, quirks and details to make the characters and their POV the centerpiece of the scene.

The Bible Thumping Religious Nut may approach with a pious stern look in their eyes.
> *I was in the midst of my Bible study, reading about the ministry throughout Galilee in the Gospel of Matthew, when I heard a screeching noise that felt like hell itself had opened and judgment day was upon us. I crossed to my stained glass window and saw through Jesus's stigmata your car possessed in the cul-de-sac burning rubber in circles. But at that moment the clouds parted and God showed me the light. Those were not circles. No. They were the devil's numbers 666 coiled together in a serpent pit of sixes. I could smell the smoke and fire and feel the clawing sound of shrieking demons. I want your son to be a penitent boy. He must confess, then march to school with the mailbox slung on his shoulder for all to judge and shame. Then and only then will he be forgiven in my eyes and the eyes of our Lord.*

An Inspired Artist may knock on the door with a totally different stance.
> *I was in the middle of making sand art for my Etsy clients when I heard this curious circular sound, almost like a low Gregorian chant, a soul-quaking meditative grumble, like the hatching of a happening, the birth of inspiration. I did what any one would do, I tried drawing what I heard with acrylics. When I peeked out the window, I was dumbstruck by the imagist haiku before me — A driverless car, rubber and road smoke and growl going nowhere fast. And then bang: an iconoclast of Americana crashing against Americana, the car and the mailbox, the piston and the cave. I was moved to tears, then I saw your child scramble from behind the wheel. I now understand Picasso's desire to draw like a child, I want to create like an infant and paint like a fetus. Please let your child know that their work was seen and heard and received and appreciated and should be enwreathed in laurels*

INFINITE WANTS

Comedy chases infinity, the horizon, the Road Runner, and our own tail. It's a terrible thing to want something, but it's what makes us most human. When our characters have desires, our scenes have heart, weight, and something to unpack inside ourselves.

Why do we want the things we want? Our desires inspire, excite and infuriate us. Once we know what a character wants, our response is binary.

Imagine the ball just dropped and Grandma wants a New Year's Kiss. If we heighten to negative infinity we will deny and distance the character from what they want.

> GRANDMA: *It's New Year's Eve, give Grandma a kiss.*

The scene partner hugs Grandma.

> GRANDMA: *I don't want a hug. I'm eighty-six years old, and this may be my last New Year's.*

The scene partner pats Grandma on the head.

> GRANDMA: *Don't pet me like a dog! Your Grandpa died nine years ago. You don't think I'm lonely?*

The scene partner laughs and gives Grandma a side hug.

> GRANDMA: *What's that? Side hug! I see you three days a year. This house is so empty. And I get a side hug!*

Now imagine the same scenario but this time we heighten to positive infinity granting the character what they want.

> GRANDMA: *It's New Year's Eve, give Grandma a kiss.*

The scene partner kisses Grandma on her forehead.

> GRANDMA: *I want one on the lips. I'm eighty-six years old, and this may be my last New Year's.*

The scene partner gives Grandma a quick peck on the lips.

> GRANDMA: ***With meaning! Your Grandpa died nine years ago. You don't think I'm lonely?***

The scene partner kisses Grandma with meaning.

> GRANDMA: ***No tongue? I see you three days a year. This house is so empty. Give me some sugar.***

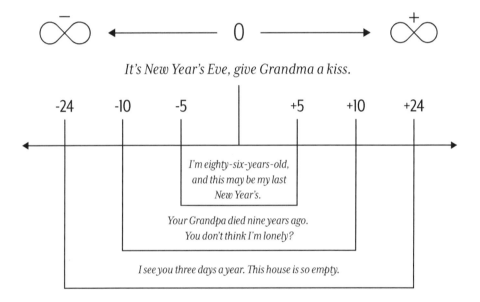

Both approaches allow the character to share their motivation and reasoning. However, even when flooded with the very thing they want, it'll never be enough. Hungry ghosts desperately eat but are never full, never happy, because there is an infinite emptiness inside of them that their wants won't satisfy.

LOVE LANGUAGES

Imagine it is late November and a six-year-old struggles to button her four-year-old sister's pea coat. This is an act of service. The younger sister thanks and hugs her older sister. Small interactions like these, early in life, form these inclinations. These *give* and *receive* combinations are planted in their hearts, affecting behavior, specificity, and future relationships.

Identifying a character's love language, the way they like to give and receive love is a huge gift. It allows players to unpack their love on a granular level.

 There are five love languages: Acts of Service, Gifts, Time, Touch, and Words of Affirmation.

Framing these coded proclivities for love as a language is essential. Unfortunately, some loving relationships feel empty because the partners don't speak the same language. No matter how much someone enunciates in Dutch that they love someone, unless that someone speaks Dutch they won't fully understand. The message will never be clear, and that's the fun. All the gifts in the world won't accomplish what a few words of affirmation could. Without a kindred match, overtures are unappreciated and ineffective and the tragedy of this builds tension and comedy.

ACTS OF SERVICE: Whether it's unclogging a drain, preparing lunch, taking out the recycling, putting together Ikea furniture, or going grocery shopping, these are acts of service. Played for comedy, a character might act like a workhorse, doing task after task, never resting, working themselves to the bone in the name of love, hoping eventually their efforts will be acknowledged.

> PLAYER A: *I'm exhausted. I can't wait to get home and go to bed.*
> ACT OF SERVICE PLAYER: *Well, here, let me drive home so you can rest. I took care of the garbage — it's already at the curb — and I'll walk the dog when we get home and you'll be happy to know I changed the sheets and made the bed so you can go right to sleep.*

GIFTS: Whether it's a diamond and sapphire encrusted tennis bracelet or a Dunkin' Donuts gift card, showering loved ones with gifts speaks volumes for the giver who may not have any words at all. A character may spend and spend, tanking their bank account to bury their loved one in things like singing telegrams, waffle irons, French bulldogs and trips to Disney gifting to the nth degree but never actually communicating their love — one million arrows aimed at the wrong target.

> PLAYER A: *I'm exhausted. I can't wait to get home and go to bed.*
> GIFTS PLAYER: *Well, then, you're in for a treat. I've got you some blackout shades from Amazon and a whale song CD along with a cooling pillow made of bamboo. Psst, Wake up! I also got you earplugs.*

TIME: Cherishing every minute and moment together, prioritizing and giving your undivided attention to each other. Time is not only of the essence, it is the essence of love. Played for comedy, a character is claustrophobic, suffocated by their partner's lust for time. They demand to share Google calendars to spend every waking moment together.

> PLAYER A: *I'm exhausted. I can't wait to get home and go to bed.*
> TIME PLAYER: *What?? You're going to bed? No, No, No, stay up, keep me company. I want to hang out. I can't believe you want to close your eyes and go to sleep like that. Do y ou have any idea how offensive that is to me? I'll come and sit in bed with you to keep you company until you wind down.*

TOUCH: [Warning: This love language demands a level of comfort and trust from the consenting scene partners.] Any PDA, hugging, hand holding, nuzzling, spooning, necking, or in a more demure 1800s fashion kinesthetically walking in step with someone to feel physically close or affectionate uses touch and proximity to show they care. Players are self-indulgent, pleasure-seeking, lotus-eating hedonists. It's less creepy when we match this energy playing the scene as two peas in a pod; think Rachel Dratch and Will Ferrell hot tubbing.

> PLAYER A: *I'm exhausted. I can't wait to get home and go to bed.*
> TOUCH PLAYER: *I know you're tired, but when we get home I'll give you a whisper massage that will invigorate your spine and awaken your libido. (They grab the person's hand as they are driving and lick their finger.) Ooh, I can still taste the garlic hummus on your fingers. You dirty girl.*

WORDS OF AFFECTION: When they bathe their scene partner in compliments and aphorisms, flooding them with flirty love notes and flowery language to declare their love in poetry. Players might not be very poetic or flattering at all, *I like your skin, it's like a buttery pan cake*, but their scene partner is lovestruck by every statement, melting for the compliment.

PLAYER A: *I'm exhausted. I can't wait to get home and go to bed.*
WORDS OF AFFECTION PLAYER: *You deserve it! You work too hard, that boss of yours doesn't appreciate you and definitely that staff don't. They're lucky they have you! I wish I could hire you, spend the whole day just telling you how darn amazing you are.*

As a coach help the ensemble find the fun in playing these love languages. Talk them through each language and option as both a giver and a receiver.

CAMERA OBSCURA

The camera obscura is a pinhole camera with a piece of photographic paper inside. It makes a reverse image of whatever subject it's aimed at. To work, the subject must maintain a certain stillness. Our eyes can communicate so much; they are a pinhole to our soul if we allow ourselves to be seen and to be vulnerable.

I begin being the vulnerable one and allow the rest of the class to comment and scene-paint based on what they see in my eyes. I choose a moment from my past full of weight and significance.

I stand in front of them and hold a snapshot in my brain of this moment from my life. I do not act it out with my body. After fifteen seconds, I shake off that moment and now invite the students to share what they think, what narratives they built around me based on my eyes, and what was their read of me. What was I radiating and what were they receiving?

> *Oh, I see somebody who was left at the altar.*
> *Somebody who doesn't have money for lunch and everybody else is eating.*
> *A POW in Vietnam crouched in a cage and soldiers from some other country lower down with ropes to free their fellow countrymen but leave you behind.*

These are all very different but all valid.

I then share my story.

In fourth grade, I started taking trombone, a class that met after school on Tuesdays.

After the first class, I went out to the bus loop and waited for my mom to pick me up. I sat there with other kids as cars circled in and picked up one after another. Eventually, I was the only one left. It was winter and the sun went down. A teacher pulled up and asked if I needed a ride. I said, *No* and they left. Then another parent came by to drop kids off for indoor soccer. They asked if I was okay and I said I was fine. It started to snow. And that's the moment I held in my eyes: just staring at the bus loop watching everybody be taken and not knowing if I had been remembered.

The idea of being left behind or being left out was inside my eyes. Being a POW, or being left at the altar or not having lunch money — all ring true to those eyes. Technically, they're not one hundred percent right. But it's about getting the gist of those eyes and recognizing the feeling of fear and sadness inside of them, a lack of belonging.

Next, have everyone buddy up and take turns reading and building narratives for each other.

Now have a brave volunteer show their eyes to the room. Ask everyone to get a read on them, and imagine a scene that gives those eyes context. When someone has a clear idea, they will raise their hand. The instructor will nod, giving the player permission to join the scene. The instructor says, *Lights up*, and the scene begins with a player making an initiation that places the volunteer and their eyes in a dynamic context.

Using the example above, the player may join as a Minister.

> MINISTER: *Are you sure we don't wanna stop the ceremony? It has been nearly an hour and the bride isn't here.*

The volunteer maintains their emotional depth while adjusting to the new context. This can be challenging because once a player has an idea of what they are, they may have a hard time letting go, being malleable and adapting to the realities that have been assigned to them.

Most improv advice says to abandon whatever you have in your head to get on board with what has been declared. This exercise encourages them to hold onto that feeling and keep that truthful story in their back pocket. At some point, we will no longer have words for what it feels like to be left at the altar. We will not be able to play the scene without breaking down and when we break down we will reveal the radiated moment, the snapshot in detail.

PLAYER A: *This has been happening my whole life: college, high school dances, even my own mother forgot to pick me up from my trombone lesson. I was sitting there in the bus loop and I watched every kid's parents come and get them one by one and then it started to snow and I sat there staring at an empty bus loop. And what sucks is I want to be married to that, married to that pattern, married to being forgotten.*

Not throwing away that initial truth allows the player to tap into it giving the scene more depth and weight and analogous resonance.

Next invite three couples, A, B, and C to sit on stage. The instructor then whispers to each couple that they are in the audience of a Broadway show, and assigns them a dynamic:

A - They are on a second date, and they like each other but one person likes the play because their sibling is in it, while the other person hates the play but is trying not to show it.

B - The Director believes this show is their opus. The assistant director wants the director to give them some small sign that they are proud of their work.

C - Two people who tried out for the play have come there to hate watch the show.

They must radiate their dynamic through their eyes, as they watch the show without movement or dialogue. The rest of the class studies each couple and their body language, mannerisms, and how they sit next to each other. After thirty seconds, invite the room to explain how they interpreted the relationships.

CHARACTERIZATION - OUTSIDE IN

The way we stand, and point, and fidget and bite at our hangnails, or squint and scrunch our nose. How we crowd up on others or give way too much space. How characters carry themselves. Where they hang out. Where they work. How they dress. How they walk or dance or trudge through their daily life. The physical world shapes our characters, what they want, and how they see the world.

Specifics are essential — twist the whiskers on your chin; cover yourself in Shrek tattoos; make people take their shoes off when they come in your house; be the hardest working optometrist in Akron; walk with a limp or speak with a lisp. Odd mannerisms and idiosyncrasies are great but recognize that they are not enough to carry a scene. Let your physical self and bearings inform your character's personality, philosophy and soul. Otherwise, it's all ornaments and no tree.

CHARACTER WALTZ

Players stand in a large circle. A player walks around the perimeter, as the ensemble gifts them with three physical attributes:

> STUDENT 1: *You're dressed head to toe in black denim.*
> STUDENT 2: *You've got a scar that runs from your left eye to behind your left ear.*
> STUDENT 3: *Your skin is leathery.*

Players must assimilate these gifts, and be transformed by them. When the choices feel real and full-bodied, the player pushes their way into the center of the circle, honoring the gifts and channelling their character. They introduce themselves, share the things they love and hate, what they do for a living and offer any advice or words of wisdom they live by.

The instructor should be ready to interview characters that seem stuck.

Question 1: Where are you from?
> JASON: *Me? I was born in Blackwell, outside of Buffalo. Witch tit cold up there, all swampland and marsh. They got all these pop-up casinos from the Iroquois all along I-90.*

Question 2: What do you do?
> JASON: *I'm a fix-it guy, fix just about anything. Heck, give me a dead bird and a rubber band and I'll have it singing by morning.*

Question 3: What's your name?
> JASON: *Name's Dale Doodas. Dang stupid name. Tells you how drunk my mother must have been when she had me. Doodas. All the kids call me dumbass, then they'd beat me into the ground and call me Dirt.*

Question 4: Where'd you get that scar?

> JASON: *I took a chain to the side of the face coming out of Matamoros, so I can't hear a damn out this ear.*

Question 5: What do you love?

> JASON: *There was this girl, Marissa, in Harlingen. They got these outlet malls there and she worked at one. Rio Grande Valley. She worked at a Fossil. I don't particularly even like Fossil, but I found myself stopping there every time I'd loop by. The way them Edison bulbs light up, where you can see the inside, that was her, just this warmth and you could see right into her mind and what was going on.*

Now that this central character is established, ask others what characters might surround that person in life, and have them state the people in simple sentences.

> Frank — a giggly old guy whose garage Dale lived in for a winter two years back.
> Louise — the woman who works the register at the Sunoco he frequents.

After they've listed four of five characters, invite one of those performers to initiate a quick six-line scene with Jason as their character.

Reload and repeat this exercise, and each time invite more scenic realism. Over time, eliminate the circle and have players walk the stage. As they perform their monologue, the backline will form a half shell around them. The ensemble can speak to draw the character from one part of the stage to another waltzing from scene to scene, building environments around them. Every interaction should reveal more about the main character, helping games to be more textured and nuanced.

Instructors can add sophistication by assigning a different lens to each corner of the room. As an example, one corner houses a character that radiates from the Head chakra, others the Heart, Gut and Groin. This helps players to establish a deal of their own while playing someone else's game. The corners can also dictate how the characters relate, one corner houses Family, another corner Friends, another Co-workers and the last Enemies.

When they've played four or five scenes, pivot the exercise to now focus on a supporting character. Place them in the spotlight to monologue and surround them with new characters that orbit their life.

ROAD TRIP

Begin by having two players sit side by side; one driver and one passenger. They mirror the instructor. If the instructor lifts an eyebrow, they will lift their eyebrow; if they hunch forward with a smirk or turtle their chin to their chest, they will take on these physical traits as well. Sculpt each player into poses and physical choices different from any gifts they've played in the past.

Have both players breathe through these choices. Inspiration requires respiration. They may feel awkward or uncomfortable but that is the gift, it shouldn't be familiar. This initial pose is a keyframe. If there were one thousand pictures of your character, more than half would be in this pose. Of course, they can move, but those movements must be kept in kind and justified through the initial spine.

A spine awakens behavior, behaviors inform characterization, and when characters interact it sparks relationship.

Players often treat the physical gift as an anomaly. They'll say something stinks in the car to explain why their face is scrunched. Note that right away. This is your face. Don't explain the gift away. Rationalizations like this make the interesting thing the thing that smells. It divorces the character from their posture. This happens because players feel self-conscious to be in this weird position and instead of committing to it and making it real and truly owning it, they bail and make it a reaction to something else.

As they breathe more life into their characters and own their choices, encourage them to look at themselves and visualize. When they look at their legs, are they wearing compression socks, flip-flops, or Jimmy Choo's? Are they in purple raver shorts or a tennis skort? Do they have too many toe rings and an ankle tattoo?

Now explore the space. Don't just be an omniscient observer. Interact with the space, touch things, and ping off your environment to make discoveries about your character. Feel the staples on a janky seatbelt, open the glove box, and pull down the visor. Are there stacks of mail or parking tickets? Is the backseat pristine or littered with Wendy's wrappers? Is the car new? Is it a rental? Is your phone paired to the car or is the driver's? Put your hand out the window. How does your character feel about the wind between their fingers?

As characters feel more lived in, applaud the believability when it's there. This builds confidence in these foreign choices.

When there's a sense that they know who and how they are as individuals, encourage them to make eye contact. The moment they do, the audience will see a spark. If one character is giving off a red aura and another blue, that spark will be purple. This connection draws the audience in and often is an instant laugh. If the scene stays true to these characters and the relationship, it will have a mix of red, blue and purple moments, playing the passenger's game, the driver's game or the relationship between them — anything else is superfluous.

If the players stray from their characters have them use *I* statements, *You* statements or *We* statements, to reinvest and fortify their characters and relationship.

This exercise begins with two characters inhabiting a small car, breathing the same air, so they are certain to interact and build relationship.

No introductions are needed. Begin in media res, four hours into a road trip. They are familiar with each other. They have a past. They have pet peeves and habits. What they don't know they can assume from their scene partner's behavior.

The car is a metaphor for their scene: two players shoulder to shoulder, moving through time and space together in the same direction.

LAND, LOOK & SPEAK

Two players mill around the space, each carrying a chair. The director prompts them to begin with a snap. Immediately, they set the chairs down and sit, striking a posture that is not their own.

Make sure players do not *correct* the chairs to better face each other. This adjustment neutralizes the unusual stage picture, nullifying the inherent tension created by their spatial relationship.

Instruct the players to live in their spine and breathe in their choice.

Now, invite eye contact. In an instant, the players register their spatial relationship, the heat between them, and the weight of their circumstances. Then, players speak through their spines, giving context to the scene.

If they wait too long to speak, call it out. The moment their eyes meet the audience starts assigning meaning and making sense of the dynamic and the longer it goes unnamed by the players the more the audience begins to fall in love with their own narrative. Now the players feel pressure to out-funny the audience's imagination. Work this muscle — Land, Look and Speak. Land in your choice, Look at your scene partner, and Speak to the scene.

The players stay seated, literally sitting in their spines. This keeps the dynamic of the scene loaded. The chairs root the players to their choices. They can't walk away from that moment, look in improv cupboards for inventions or busy themselves with frantic energy that scatters focus. They are their first choices. They must invest in the reality they've created, identify what is happening and how it makes them feel, and then find ways to accentuate it.

If a player's shoulders are square with the back wall, keep them that way. A player can steal a glance here and there but if they allow their choices to melt and bend, their POV will shift as well and with it their relationship. When players move without purpose, it clouds things, which makes it harder to triangulate who they are to each other in relation to the scene.

The moment they catch each other's eyes, the scene starts, all through justification and reaction. It's liberating to play a scene that starts so *in the now*, born out of honest reactions to what is seen and felt.

When the scene dynamic and characterization solidify, allow the players to move, but only if they use their movement to add more texture to their choices, to heighten their characters or the relationship.

Next, remove the time restriction. Let the performers decide when their relationship has solidified enough for them to move about the stage.

This exercise activates pockets of the stage that performers rarely use. It awakens a playfulness for blocking and an appreciation for dynamic stage picture.

EMOTIONAL LANDMINES

Begin by drawing an invisible line partitioning stage right from left, then bisect that line between upstage and down. Now label each quadrant clearly:

Downstage Right: Happiness
Downstage Left: Sadness
Upstage Right: Anger
Upstage Left: Pity/Sympathy

Get the entire ensemble on their feet walking around the space. As they move from one quadrant to the next have them take on the corresponding emotions. Invite them to exaggerate these emotions; let them lift their spirits or sink in despair. Have them move faster from one emotional landmine to another.

Now ask for two volunteers to remain up. Everyone else takes a seat. Suggest a location that would fit on the stage, like a Frozen Yogurt Shop.

Have the two players visualize the environment. Is the toppings bar dirty? Does it need to be wiped down? Do they need to top off the Fruity Pebbles, Oreos, and Shaved Coconut? A few M&M Minis have spilled on the floor, and there's a smudge of fudge on the scale near the register. Give them time to see that one of the napkin dispensers is empty or that the flavor of the month is Horchata.

Now have them independently cross to one of the things they visualized and touch it, interact with it. If they are upstage right remind them that they will fill with anger as they clean up M&M Minis. If they are downstage left, they fill with sadness as they restock the napkins. This connects each player to the environment through their object and allows them to tap into an emotional choice based on their placement on stage. Once the players have anchored to the environment and assimilated an emotion, invite them to make eye contact and begin the scene.

One player restocks the napkins and spoons, sad. They just found out their co-worker, their scene partner, wants to quit. It makes them take stock of their own life. They are twenty-seven and have been working at this YogurtLand for the last ten years, and they're still not manager, they don't even have a key. All they have to show for themselves is carpal tunnel and pre-diabetes. They wipe away their tears with a napkin.

The other player picks up M&M Minis pissed off, fed up and tired of missing out on their teenage years working this shitty job, while other kids in their grade just get handed Land Rovers on their sixteenth birthday. They hate coming home and smelling like sour milk every night. Worse, they hate serving kids from their grade when they come in. They chuck the handful of M&Ms they picked up across the room.

If players gravitate to each other out of fear, note it when it happens. An uninspired cross sells out their initial emotional state instead of investing in it. Invite them to plant themselves where they started and stay there until their emotions take root, adding context and revealing who they are, how they see the world and how they feel about each other. Once the dynamic and relationship have emerged and heightened, then they are free to move to other parts of the stage with purpose.

These landmines give meaning to where the characters stand. They charge the scene with emotionality and give the players something to unpack and justify. The exercise motivates and rewards players to use the whole space. When they inhabit a different part of the stage, they activate different sides of themself. Motion yields emotion and these stage directions change the dynamic between characters.

A playwright's stage directions aren't an example of what could happen, they are written with intention. It doesn't read, *The sheriff crosses to the desk and throws down their badge if they feel like it.* No. In theater every line, every word and every movement is purposeful. Things don't just get moved around, players need to be moved by those things. When characters restock the FroYo store, they're taking stock of their own lives.

Intentionality is everything.

Watch for players bailing on their choices and chasing the gimmick instead of putting in the work. This reads manic, shifting from one part of the room to another without reason or context. If players don't do the work, the scene will nosedive, sending them running to another quadrant to hide. Call this out. There is no hiding on stage. They need to put in the work to grow their scenes into something substantial.

Veteran players can make ten shifts in a three-minute scene and have each one feel earned and specific, but that same player also knows when they only have to shift once.

CHARACTERIZATION - INSIDE & OUT

These exercises create wireframes mapping behavior and movement, speech and spirit to channel a character from both inside and out. Knowing a character's obsessions and possessions, their philosophy and physiology, how they angle, how they listen, how they treat others or ferret around or crow like a braggart — a character's *Who* and *How* must be played, not just stated. Walk in their shoes, groove on their logic, sharpen their point of view, finish their run-on sentences, and push past corny imitation to something more honest and intimate. Let their energy propel your motor to make like-minded discoveries and declarations through their lens.

WIRE-FRAMES

Every second of traditional animation required twenty-four separate cells to be drawn, to capture every gesture, grimace and glance. Nothing is wasted. Nothing is drawn without intentionality. Every choice has purpose. Every character has a way, a character game, a signature. The same should be true of our characters on stage. Don't just be a waiter who rocks forward off the backline, offers food and then vanishes. Be depressed, mope into the scene head hung, dragging your feet, or be jittery, over-caffeinated and short-fused. Be specific. Be grounded. Be real.

When cops are named Johnson, teachers are named Johnson, neighbors, scientists, and doctors are named Johnson — it feels fake, lazy and impersonal.

The devil's in the details.

Use your neighbors' names — DiMarco, Fix, Chernobyl, Kandilkar, Svboda, Abramowitz. Specifics stand out in a sea of Johnsons. Don't just go to a doctor, go to an ENT specialist; when the diagnosis comes, be concerned about your insurance or parking validation. Unique experiences supercharge our scenes with vibrance, truth and realness.

Help the audience see themselves or humanity in you. This exercise challenges players to be undeniably distinct and memorable, using their spine, movement and energy to create characterization.

Begin with all players up and moving around the space. Explain that you will describe various Winnie the Pooh characters, and as you do the players will take on the traits of these distinctive tropes.

WINNIE THE POOH

First, encourage the players to totter with their hips locked like an anthropomorphic stuffed bear. As they pass each other, they should radiate a good-natured friendly presence. Winnie the Pooh is a soft-spoken, slow-witted, lovable teddy bear and addict. That's the gear shift. Players must establish both sides of his personality: the loving naive friend and his impulsive, obsessive infatuation regarding all things honey. Players must demonstrate a tender-hearted gentle soul to have that derailed by their obsession, with *honey*. It's a single-minded fixation; the rest of the world, his friends, and his safety melts away along with any reason.

Now invite someone to initiate a scenario with Winnie energy: a coach of a little league huddles up with their team. They cheer and give an uplifting speech to boost morale, but in the middle of their speech, they smell watermelon bubble gum and become absolutely obsessed and thrown off course.

PIGLET

Have everyone move on tiny cloven feet, with unsure steps. As they pass each other they are equal parts curious and cautious. Piglet's spirit for adventure is at odds with his extreme worrywart tendencies. He's anxiety-ridden and lacks self-esteem. Playing someone this nervous and scared realistically can be a trap. They'd never go anywhere or do anything. Instead, have players take on the comedic reality of this energy. Nose into trouble, don't outsmart it to win. It's boring to go to a show where the characters are afraid to fail, where they make the sensible choice, where it's all reward and no risks.

> **Side Note:** *Tommy Boy* starring Chris Farley and David Spade is a great example. Tommy is a spoiled frat boy. When his father dies leaving their Brake Pad company in limbo, the most rational tactic would've been to get all the company's most savvy salespeople on the phone to assure their clients that they are in good hands; problem solved, everyone wins, credits roll. But that is not funny. It's boring. Do the wrong thing with the best intentions. Go against your better judgment. Remember, it's fun to torture your characters. Send them on a fool's errand. Let Piglet-y characters nose into danger, then panic and fret over it all. They are scared but interested. Their interest overrides their fear which leads to discoveries that can awaken more fear and anxiety.

Now invite someone to initiate a scenario with Piglet energy: a wide-eyed nineteen-year-old from Arkansas gets off a bus in Las Vegas. Everything excites them. They are drawn to the lights, the performers, the fountains, the spectacle, but also scared out of their minds that their pockets will be picked, the fillings stolen from their teeth, and their kidneys cut out of their backs.

OWL

Have everyone puff out their chest with their arms behind their back and their feet turned out and touching at the ankle. The challenge is to occupy as little space on the ground as possible but take up as much above the waist as possible. This posture at a standstill feels distinguished, high-ranking, and even regal. Now have them flap their arms to move, clumsy and bumbling about. This is Owl energy. He's revered and wise but also bumbling, the absent-minded professor who gets lost in his thesis. Every conversation turns into a dissertation. As players pass each other, they bloviate, pontificate. Think of your wings as the academic regalia of your doctoral robe. Flap and gesticulate as though there are visual aids all around.

Owl is very much a head chakra. Their body is used to bumble their brain from place to place. Every iota of focus goes into making points with microscopic tunnel vision but missing the big picture.

The fun of this character is in allowing yourself to be an idiot savant, an eccentric genius: the professor who knows everything about neuroscience but is oblivious to the fact that mud is splattered up their back from their butt to their neck from having biked to school.

Now invite someone to initiate a scenario with Owl energy, ideally not in a classroom: a museum guide leads a tour through the Uffizi, accidentally knocking vases off pedestals, breaking statues, staining tapestries, and punching a hole through Sandro Botticelli's The Birth of Venus.

Remind players they are not bound to make actual sense. No one will fact-check their claims. This should liberate them. What matters most is that they allow themselves to talk themselves in circles, eddying on a single notion until their run-ons spring to a new stream of consciousness. Don't let anyone be afraid of saying something stupid. Stupid is the fun of this character. They are the myopic sage, a bird-brained genius with their head in the clouds who thinks everything they say is groundbreaking.

TIGGER

Have players bounce and bound around the room with joy and enthusiasm. Have them pass each other as hyperactive social magnets full of spontaneity looking for fun. Tigger spends most of his time bouncing, yelling *Hoo-hoo-hoo*. Underline the importance of this. When players jump they can't zig or zag; there's no pivot until they land, until they come back down to earth. Tigger rarely has both his feet set firmly on the ground; sometimes he's just balancing on his tail. He'd rather be bouncing than standing anchored in reality. So he bounds into trouble and chaos and fun, making brash decisions with scissors in his hands. He acts first and thinks later or maybe not at all. Tigger's good-spirited energy is simple and animalistic. Live for the day.

Encourage players to bounce into conversations laughing with gusto, to be a catalyst percolating with restlessness. They're short-attention span thrill seeker with a joyful heart, who may sign checks that the rest of the group has to cash.

Now invite someone to initiate a scenario with irrepressible Tigger energy: someone who shows up late to a family Fourth of July picnic with cocaine, then eats all the ambrosia and barfs it up on a child, before setting off a Roman candle between their butt cheeks.

KANGA

Have players close their eyes to still and center themselves, invite them to square their shoulders with their hips, anchor their feet, then guide them to breathe and radiate warmth from their hearts and let that kindness, sympathy and hospitality emanate. This is Kanga energy. Feel the love in your veins, use your arms to hug and swaddle. She's welcoming and inclusionary.

Now have the players open their eyes and cross to each other, babying one another.

Some players write this nurturing, mothering energy off as *un-fun* and boring. They're wrong. Help them see past that mental block. Shower teammates with hand-made scarves and mittens and quilts, cherish each other with pride, be concerned and compelled to connect, overjoyed and verklempt, and when you say goodbye go back for one more hug and another. Every moment is a memento; treasure every interaction for keepsakes and souvenirs.

Now invite someone to initiate a scenario with Kanga energy: a kindergarten teacher who cares and consoles too much. They mother and smother to the nth degree as a roided up helicopter mom flattening anyone or anything in their *students'* path.

RABBIT

Ask the players to tap their feet, impatient. Now have them scrunch their nose with disgust, then shift their weight from side to side. Even in their own skin invite them to be unsettled and fidgety. This is Rabbit energy, OCD and antsy, always working or stressed, obsessed with order and putting things in rows and columns and lines. They are so persnickety about perfection that they look strung out, worn and frayed, about to snap. As players pass each other encourage them to arrange the furniture in the room to their taste. Tidy up. Knit-pick each other. Insist everything be to their standards and no one else's. Be fed up and territorial. Shoulder in on conversations, correct grammar, be unrelentingly crotchety and opinionated with a rake up your butt.

Now invite someone to initiate a scene with stressed and obsessed Rabbit energy: a family portrait photographer at J.C. Penney who keeps repositioning the children. There are only two ways to do something: their way and the wrong way.

EEYORE

Ask the players to imagine an invisible yoke around their neck, its heft breaking their spirit and spine, pulling their chin below their chest. They sway side to side trudging, lumbering slowly through slop. This is Eeyore energy. His depressed melancholia teeters on catastrophe. This thistle-eating donkey is profoundly conflicted and undeniably human. He wants love but struggles to give or receive it. He's an outsider, lonely, living in a gloomy place, boggy and sad. He spends all his time sinking in thought, drowning in *Why*, detached from others. Why Eeyore? Eeyore isn't a name, it's a noise, a braying bark. Why? Is he unworthy of a name, is he just that beastly, or unimportant or unloved? The more he questions and reflects, the more depressed he becomes. Life is a slog. Nothing comes easy or fast. He carries the world on his back, bursting at his seams, his tail nailed to him. Only sarcasm buoys him from these existential woes, but all irony is lost, over the heads of his friends. Yet he's loyal, dependable and will slog through anything for them.

Now invite someone to initiate a scenario with Eeyore energy: a wedding planner who's late to the appointment because their car ran out of gas. They are sweaty and wheezing. They have albums slung over their shoulder and another being dragged behind them. They need help even turning the pages because their carpal tunnel is so bad. They wince in pain just looking at their hands. They have a whole spiel about the beauty and power of marriage but they themselves were stood up at the altar.

Next instruct players to revisit each character. As they bound around brash with Tigger energy, talk over this, ask them to think about how buoyant they are, how impulsive, and what kinds of choices flow out of them when they're radiating through this character lens. Now shift to Kanga. Call out how the room changes from wild to grounded and nurturing. Shift again to Rabbit: obsessed with order futzing with the chairs, cantankerous and always a hair away from giving up on the world. Then switch to Eeyore, Piglet, Owl and Pooh. These quick hit callbacks help players reinforce these choices in their bones.

Next, have two volunteers up. They secretly choose one of these characters as a wireframe for their scene: Rabbit and Piglet. Now gift them with a relationship between two people like a Stylist and a Celebrity. They will use their wireframe to bring behavior, dimension and consistency to their characters. A Rabbity OCD stylist preparing their nervous Piglet client for a gala. This adds depth to their character's sense of self.

If you've seen Pixar's *The Incredibles* there's a scene where Mr. Incredible is being fired from his Life Insurance job. He's called to his boss's office. The scene begins with the boss sharpening a pencil, exacting. He then sets it on a desk calendar perfectly parallel with others. When Mr. Incredible sits the floor quakes and the pencils roll out of order and his boss immediately puts them back in place. This tiny detail elevates the character. From behavior alone, before the boss even speaks, we know that he is infuriated with Mr. Incredible. In lesser hands this is a throwaway character with zero dimension; they'd only exist to forward the plot by firing Mr. Incredible. However, Brad Bird uses a Rabbit wireframe to establish the boss's affinity for order: he rants about efficiencies, fastidious and fussy until Mr. Incredible snaps and throws the boss through four cubicle walls.

SCRIPTED BEHAVIOR

This exercise traces acclaimed scenes from plays to create analogous beats. This approach focuses less on creation and more on channeling and playing within a defined role. Many performers can understand how a character functions. They see their speech patterns and habits. They can read their status and levels of desperation and even take on those qualities and harness those choices to make discoveries.

Begin with two particularly strong performers on stage seated in chairs. Hand each a copy of David Mamet's *Glengarry Glen Ross*. Have them turn to the opening scene between Levene and Williamson and read aloud. It's a cold read but invite them to act the hell out of it.

The first page may be wonky, but once they give over to the tempo and cadence of the characters the language will guide them. Its rhythm has an almost trance-like power, swirling like a riptide pulling the reader under its spell. It helps the players and the audience see the world the way the characters see the world, whether it's beautiful or grotesque or sniping or precious. Their worldview becomes our worldview. Their word choice becomes ours.

The rest of the class just listens. After five to eight minutes, call scene. Ask for thoughts. What did they like? What worked? Then, what do they know about these characters? Are they analytical and straightforward, panicked or sniveling? Ask them to look at the language. Look at the way characters speak, the way they listen, and how they treat each other or react. What words do they remember? What about sentence length or structure? Levene speaks in a desperate never-ending run-on, snaking and taking every angle he can, relentless, while Williamson is absolutely fed up and fights to interject with details, facts and fragments.

Ask, what's important? What's happening and what is actually happening here? Don't rush past their remarks. Hear everyone out. Unpack their observations as revelations. Hopefully, they see that characters are so much more than a goofy spine and weird voice. Good characterization has rhythm, a heartbeat, and a soul. When performers tap into that they can sail on that wave of energy to make like-minded moves that align with their logic.

How a character talks is as important as what they say, if not more.

Next, have the same two players channel their characters to create an analogous beat. Assign them a scenario: a Girl Scout Troop leader (Levene) wants the regional manager (Williamson) to give their troop a better neighborhood. Encourage them to use everything that was discussed, mirror the speech patterns and emulate Levene's whining and angling strategies, while Williamson is all business, calling out every one of Levene's points for the excuses they are. The set-up and specifics are different, but the desperation and characterization are the same.

ANIMALISTIC BEHAVIOR

Begin with everyone moving around the space. Prompt them to jump like a frog. With each hop, the players transform, more amphibious. Their head, face, chin and torso bunch, short and squat, while their legs lengthen, their skin dampens and gets slippery. Invite realism.

When performers can't use words to show off their wit, they feel exposed and uncomfortable. Words are a crutch. Players say their ideas, boss their scene partners around, and give orders to feel comfortable. When words are taken away, some panic, and start sniping and selling out the exercise. They'll make two-dimensional choices and act extra silly — it's their defense mechanism, a form of ironic detachment. Call it out. Explain that this is their ego trying to protect them, because by half-committing they can never fully fail, but if they aren't willing to fail then they will never fully grow.

Commit. Dare to be stupid. Dare to be vulnerable. Dare to learn and grow.

Celebrate the players accepting the challenge. Underline the verisimilitude, the micro-details honoring the animal, capturing spirit, and nuance. Have the players move like square-eyed baby goats, then eels, and weasels; smooth-haired long-horned gazelles; fast and clumsy three-toed emus; Okefenokee Swamp mosquitos, etc. Strive for National Geographic levels of authenticity.

Embodying these animals awakens musculature, gives new uses for knuckles, contorts the neck, and reinvigorates arms and legs.

Next, have everyone sit in a large circle. Invite two players up in the center and assign them each an animal to inhabit. Ideally, these are animals that would be an unlikely match as friends such as a Barn Owl and a Shetland Pony. Help players avoid stock adversarial choices like cat and dog. Suggest symbiotic relationships like the Hippo and the Oxpecker, where the birds eat ticks and parasites off the hippo's body. The hippo gets free grooming while the birds get free food.

The goal is not to play a scene so much as to channel the spirit of these animals, their movement, their tempo, their soul, and exist as they would in truth. A squirrel may dart through the space patting acorns in the ground with quick careful hands before scurrying somewhere else. A silverback might lift their head and close their eyes to bask in the September sun. Whatever the pairing, players want to be genuine with their behaviors while also clocking their scene partner's choices, and reacting to them through their lens.

If a bobcat stalks closer to a star-nosed mole, the mole may startle up, listening, intently. Animal behavior is so rich and real, that very little needs to happen in these moments. Don't force narrative. Two lions can sleep on top of each other, lazily, and that's enough. Maybe one paws at another to get comfortable, then settles lying there, just breathing alongside the other.

After each scene, ask the audience of Jane Goodalls seated around them for moments they loved. When a particularly resonant and beautiful scene occurs, ask the players to repeat the scene. They'll hit the same marks, the same moments with the same behavior, only this time as humans with the spirit of that animal inside them.
If the squirrel darted downstage, the human will dart downstage. This is essentially a behavioral second beat. The first scene blazes a path for the players to reprise and pattern with an analogous kindred spirit that honors the same simplicity and soul, but as humans and with language if needed.

Now the human character zags downstage with squirrelly energy, scurrying about to pack a suitcase, patting it down with careful hands. The star-nosed mole becomes a near-sighted security guard on the graveyard shift at a storage warehouse, listening intently for any funny business. The lions become two parents having their first lazy Sunday since their child was born, lounging all day content in bed.

The track work has been set. Players know their behavior, their How, and their relationship to their scene partner, their Function. This puts players' bodies in front of their minds, giving them a running start into their second beats. They have blocking, spatial relationship, behavior and spine. These elements need to be contextualized through a new human lens. This requires justification and reinvestment more than invention.

Players may fall into a trap by scripting in their heads an analogous beat. Having a context as a starting point is fine, but clinging to that context, forcing the scene to be played by their script, their vision, their rules, and their reality, is dangerous. Make it clear that whatever context is established first is the reality to be played. Beyond that the players need to let go of any other scripted specifics they had in mind and simply return to their How and their Function and be present.

Challenge players to fold in animalistic quirks, calls, and mannerisms to their human counterparts. An aarfing sea lion can easily become a car salesman honking horns, clapping, leading with their nose, full of charisma. This can be dialed down and full of subtlety or extremely broad, but every choice should be consistent.

SHORT-FORM FORMATS

Short-form is transparent. The audience can see the mechanics, the crowd-sourcing, and the players contorting to incorporate the slips of paper and weave them into their scenes. Every few moments, with every new game and suggestion, the audience is reaffirmed that this is entirely unplanned.

A great short-form set feels like an Olympic floor routine, listing out exactly what the players will do and then watching them deliver those things masterfully. Audiences know what to expect and they love the gymnastics of it all and watching the performers stick the landing.

Short-form games are also perfect for sourcing scene drills and exercises for lesson plans.

UP THE MOUNTAIN

Begin with five players. They'll take a suggestion and one player will start a solo scene. When that scene crests, that player will be joined for a new two-person scene. When that scene crests, that duo will be joined for a new three-person scene. Then that trio will be joined for a new four-person scene. Then those four players will be joined for a new five-person scene.

On the way up the mountain, 1-2-3-4-5, invite players to make five distinct initiations off the same suggestion. This way the piece truly explores the suggestion from many angles.

The five-person scene will heighten to its end, then the fifth player will peel off, and the remaining four players will revisit their four-person scene, the fourth player will peel off to revisit the three-person scene, and so on back to one.

This format is commonly played for quick justifications as a fun short-form game. However, the same mechanics approached with patient scene work fuel long form formats like JTS Brown or Four Square.

Typically, the player entering initiates as they have a better vantage for identifying what the piece needs. For example, after an emotionally charged monologue, it might be nice to chase that with something physical and light. With each entrance, players can abandon their current stage picture to field the next initiation. A more complex option would have players justify their stage picture when that entrance happens. Both are valid, but justification with newer players has a tendency to become too loony and over-shadows the initiation, muddying the game.

Going down the mountain, 5-4-3-2-1, justification is a must. Imagine - four players searching through the wreckage of a tornado. They turn over a chair, desperate to find their laptop, car keys or the 24-pack of Diet Doctor Pepper they just bought. A player wanders off to check the neighbor's yard and instantly the chair on its side becomes a Great Dane giving birth, then one of the three players runs off to get a beach towel for the puppies, and the remaining two dive behind the chair taking cover in a Paintball tournament. Immediate re-contextualization adds intricacy as players pivot from one reality to another, tumbling back to their solo scene.

This format thrives on stage picture. If players stand center stage and only say their games, this format will be dead on arrival. It needs movement and action to fuel discoveries.

On the way up the mountain, players must establish meaningful relationships, with bold characters and clear wants. If they don't know who they are on the way up the mountain, chances are they won't know who they are on the way down and neither will the audience. Emphasize the importance of knowing and showing who and how they are through behavior so that on the way down, each revisit can be sharper, more distilled and more compelling.

Rehearsing this format keeps players sharp for pivot edits used in any long form that has second beats or culminates with an avalanche of callbacks.

WHAT'S MY LINE??

Begin by having two players leave the room. A host fields suggestions from the audience: What's your favorite movie quote? Favorite song lyric? The last text someone sent you? The best or worst piece of advice you've ever received? etc.

These answers are jotted on slips of paper. The players are invited back and each takes three slips of paper and blindly puts them in their pocket. The players are given a relationship between two people such as Robber and Applebee's daytime manager.

Once the scene has taken off and is cruising, a player will read a slip of paper from their pocket. *Do or do not, there is no try.* No matter how ill-fitting and nonsensical the absurd, poetic, left-field statements might be, the Robber must justify and commit to them, folding them into their character's logic and worldview seamlessly.

This game is perfect for players who are too safe and struggle to cede control. These rogue statements force players out of their own logic and comfort zones. Some players read the line but gloss over it. Invite them to embrace the need for justification. Treat every line as sacred text written by a playwright. Why would a robber quote Yoda? Give the character a tattoo over their heart of Darth Vader and Luke locked in battle with their light sabers. Their getaway car has a bumper sticker that reads *My other ride is a pod racer.* Their dad was a gambler who went over to the Dark Side and left his family high and dry after betting away the mortgage to their double wide.

Understanding a character's *Why?* gives them motivation and informs their behavior.

In real life, we tell ourselves we're doing something for one reason, but ultimately it's to justify our own existence, to matter, to be seen, to have power, or at least to feel powerful.

Our Why is like an onion. We may think that we need money but if we ask why, we figure out that it's for vanity. And if we ask Why again, we realize that it's for acceptance. And if we dig below that, it's because we always felt like an outsider even in our own family. And if we ask again we realize ... it can go on and on.

We need to strengthen this justifying muscle. Otherwise, our rationales are clichéd, saccharine, surface-level, shallow explanations. They ring fake and ridiculous. If we do not tap into something universal and truthful then this creates a hollowness in our characters and the audience will always see them as mannequins, empty puppets.

HITCHHIKERS

Begin by setting four chairs to create the semblance of a car driving toward the audience. Ask for a volunteer who likes to sing to sit in the driver's seat. Then choose three performers who will enter as passengers.

The progression of the scene begins with the driver, Player A, singing a song as they drive. If it's sad, belt out the sadness of the song. If it's a GoGo's song, enjoy being cheerful. When the driver has had time to create an emotionally charged base reality, the instructor will cue the first hitchhiker to enter with their thumb out.

Players new to this exercise will milk this interaction, asking way too many questions. What's their name? Where are they going? How much are they willing to chip in for gas? Skip the formalities; have the first hitchhiker jump into the car with a defined sense of self. Instantly, their energy, their whole M.O. will bewitch the driver, so they both now have the same behaviors, thoughts, feelings and viewpoints.

If the first passenger is paranoid, then the driver will be too. They'll feed off each other's conspiracies and concerns. They'll check their mirrors and take sharp turns to shake any cars that might be tailing them. Their shared paranoia should mount and mount, more dangerous and just before the scene crests — a second hitchhiker will enter with their thumb out.

Note: If they were honoring their paranoia and playing it *real* they'd likely never pull the car over; they'd floor it and get as far away from them as possible. But it's always more fun to play the comedic reality of these scenes — Chunk from *Goonies* is a great example. He spends the entire movie telling the gang that they should turn back and go home: **Guys, if we don't get out of here soon, there's gonna be some kind of hostage crisis. Out in the garage, ORV, four-wheel drive bullet holes the size of matzo balls.** He's the holy fool and voice of reason saying *No* at every turn throughout the adventure, but continuing along the quest. The paranoid couple in the car can do the same.

DRIVER: *I don't like the looks of this guy!*
BRIAN: *They've got hungry eyes. Why are we stopping?*
DRIVER: *This does not bode well. I regret this already.*

The players allow the hitchhiker to supercharge their concern yet still pull over the car for them to get in.

The second hitchhiker, Charlie, wastes no time and hops in. Their declarative hopeless romantic energy instantly bewitches the others, so now all three share this point of view, smitten with every person they pass, and in love with each other.

A third and final hitchhiker, Danielle, stands with her thumb out. The car stops. Danielle drags her feet, moping as she gets in the car. She whines.

DANIELLE: *It's not worth living anymore.*

Instantly everyone in the car adopts this bleak outlook. As the four continue to heighten this mood the driver stops steering and says,

DRIVER: *This steering wheel is pointless. I'm not driving this car, it's driving me.*

They all unbuckle their seat belts.

BRIAN: *Chaos, do your worst.*

Another opens their door hanging their head inches from the road, wishing to end it all. As the car speeds faster, Danielle makes a grim statement and then somersaults out of the back seat.

The moment they leave, the car instantly snaps back to the hopeless romantic game, commenting on Danielle's tragic exit.

CHARLIE: *Am I crazy? I mean I know she just dove face-first onto asphalt but I feel like maybe she just wanted me to notice her.*
BRIAN: *Like maybe she wanted you to fix her!*
CHARLIE: *Guys, what if that was my soul mate?*
DRIVER: *Go to her!*
BRIAN: *But wait, what if you're the love of my life?*

CHARLIE: *Oh dang. What if we're all the loves of each other's lives?!*
DRIVER: *Shh, don't tell me your name!*
CHARLIE: *Don't tell me your number!*
BRIAN: *If we are meant to be …*
CHARLIE: *Then the universe will put us in each other's lives again. Au revoir!*
DRIVER: *Until we meet again!*

Here the players hit one last cymbal crash of the *Hopeless Romantic* game before they exit.

The moment they're gone, the car snaps back to the paranoid conspiracy theorists' game.

BRIAN: *Hit the gas! Go! Go! Go!*
DRIVER: *Get as far away from that psycho as possible. I don't trust them!*

Be super sharp with these games. Reacting to other character's exits lets players springboard back to their character's game with efficiency.

DRIVER: *I didn't trust them from the moment we picked them up!*
BRIAN: *You're lying!*
DRIVER: *You're lying!!*
BRIAN: *Wait, how do I know you're not going to drive us off a cliff?!*

Brian tries to wrestle the wheel from the driver. They fight.

BRIAN: *I knew you couldn't be trusted!*
DRIVER: *Get out of my car!!*

The driver kicks the passenger out of the speeding car and the door slams shut. Instantly the driver turns the volume back up and continues to sing their song as the lights fade.

Hitchhiker is all about being the epitome of our ideas. It thrives on clarity and shows the power of glomming onto the fun of each others' choices. It is a great ramp-in to *Monoscenes* which require players to make a powerful entrance. Players want to kick down the door with energy and enthusiasm for everyone to rally around. Hit character games with all the firepower you have, then exit with authority on a high note, hitting your game one last time, without overstaying your welcome.

Novice players are instructed to drop old behaviors for the new ones instantly. However, the more familiar players are with this format the more nuanced they can be. Instead of snapping to the new behavior, hold on to the previous one and let the new behavior slowly spread through the car, infecting the scene. This makes the transition feel less game-y and more earned.

To play a character's game, players must understand the character's logic, motivation, and emotional state. This exercise allows ensembles to surf on each other's wavelengths, walk in each other's shoes, and empathize through assimilation. It trains players not to be too territorial about their worldview or their characters'. Our gifts are gifts for the group to share. The more ensemble members inhabit each other's characters and points of view, the more familiar they will be when playing a non-matching scene with this character type in the future.

NEW CHOICE

Two players begin with a prompt and build a scene. At any point, the director can yell, *New Choice!* and the player last to speak must rewind, retracting their last declaration and offering a totally new one in its place.

> LAUREN: *I need to get home because it's dinner time.*

New Choice.

> LAUREN: *I need to get home ... because the purge is about to begin, and I don't want to get trapped roaming the streets when murder is legal.*

New Choice

> LAUREN: *I need to get home ... tonight's game seven of the NBA finals.*

Every second on stage is full of infinite possibilities. Players might know where they'd like to take a scene. They may have a hope for where it goes, but they can't cling to that hope. There is no hope in improv, only declarations.

This exercise demands players be an *Anding* machine, an un-judging endless waterfall of declarations. It trains their creative brain to be nimble, hopping from one idea to the next, without ego, sulking or hesitation. They have to commit to whatever oddball choice is made with zero irony and 100% commitment.

As an instructor, don't sacrifice the scene for the gimmick. It's tempting because people rattling off robust specifics is a crowd pleaser, but the primary directive is to have a scene people care about. When kooky choices are stacked on weirder choices chasing laughs, it all starts to feel flat and self-serving.

Some players are genius at coming up with things. It's effortless. But if a player is too exceptional, too clever, too at ease, there's no sweat, no fear, no risk. Remember it's still a show. Players need to frame the danger up top to dazzle the audience later.

Trapeze artists know this. When they perform their meticulous routine, they intentionally wobble or slip at the start to invite danger into the tent. This makes the audience gasp and buy into the risk, the stakes get bigger, and the tightrope narrows and heightens. This primes the audience to be all the more astonished by their skill.

Even though the host seems like they are out to stump the players, remember they are working in concert with the players to build a great scene. They must use the gimmick sparingly to surprise the players and the audience. They want a healthy ratio of solid scene work to chaos. Directors must not capsize the scene with too many commands. Only when players stabilize the scene, is it time to rock the boat again by demanding a new choice.

PILLARS

The mechanics of this short-form game require two players on stage flanked by two pillars, audience participants, standing on stage right and left. As the improvisers build a grounded two-person scene they tap a pillar on the shoulder and the audience member provides that player with their next line of dialogue. The player repeats the random line with absolute commitment. No matter how senseless the offer is, the two players must justify and make sense of it.

Insist players avoid rationales that explain away the offer's intrinsic absurdity: *I'm sorry. I'm not sure why I said that. It must be time for my pills.* This distances their character from the gift. It explains away the fun and creates a logical reason for the chaos but does not take ownership of it. Instead, double down on the non-sequitur and make audiences believe you meant to say it. Build a case and justify through behavior. Own the line, don't apologize for it. Fun-chasing improvisers roll out the red carpet for trouble, instead of sweeping it under the rug. Improvisers' brains relish mistakes and lawlessness; which give players something to police and the piece an element of risk. Pillars is designed to be a turbo button. It forces players to let go, and be weird and awaken their sense of play.

There's a difference between an airport and an airshow.

Improv needs to be daring. It needs surprises. Audiences come to an air show to watch two planes nose dive at each other, nearly grazing wings at blazing speeds, not to land an airbus in Newark right on time. If players are in control of every moment on stage then they aren't risking anything, they're auto-piloting, and they probably aren't growing.

Reframe entropy as an opportunity, a necessity for growth. Otherwise, the player's ego will protect them from it. It stops them from making mistakes, from failing, and steers them along the safest routes, toward the familiar and away from turbulence. This is uninspiring to watch.

The instinct of self-preservation is tough to break. Controlling players may struggle and squirm when they hand over the reins and let others decide what they say. They'll buck and ignore additions that challenge their perception of the scene. Note it immediately. Unchecked, these controlling tendencies can fester. If a player is this fanatical, remove the pillars and add a new rule. Whenever the instructor points at this player, they must speak in gibberish. They can carry on as though they're making sense with emotion, but their words will have no power. Their scene partner will then interpret their gibberish. Right or wrong, the player must accept their offers, surrendering their control to the scene and their teammates.

When a player allows others to put words in their mouth, it's a chance to think outside themselves. It's an invitation to grow and rewire themselves for success.

TED EXPERTS

Two players receive an esoteric thesis topic for a suggestion: Trevi Fountain, Zodiac Killer, WWE 2002-2006, Knot Theory, etc. The duo will then deliver a keynote speech to the audience as authorities on the subject.

The players are charlatan flimflam artists, and their job is to swindle the audience into believing in the nonsense they're selling. Invite players to radiate from the head chakra with distinction, gift themself with prestigious credentials and accolades, and endorse each other as luminaries in their field.

If players shrink and seem clueless, call it out. Players stall for time, scrambling for the right words because they want to be right. They want to look smart. They fear failing and sounding dumb or being seen as a fraud. But that is the real assignment. Audiences don't expect a scholarly lecture. No one wants factuality. They want fake facts with one hundred and ten percent commitment. They want to see the duo navigate a complex minefield together and make it through not by their knowledge but by their ingenuity.

How a character speaks matters more than what they say. If players aren't buying what they're saying, neither will the audience. Play to the top of your intelligence. Steer the presentation to things you know. Leverage keywords to speak in metaphors with meaning as opposed to aimless drivel.

Sometimes luck has it that a player will know hard facts about the suggestion, and they'll want to prove they know what they know, leaving their scene partner floundering. A player's desire to connect should outweigh their desire to show off. If they huff and roll their eyes at their partner's inaccuracies, it breeds judgment. Note this — players must keep in alignment with their partner and cheer their offers even when they make zero sense, to stay on the same toboggan together. When we treat our scene partner as a cancer, it kills the presentation. Instead, treat their bizarre offers as a light-ning bolt of genius. Frame ridiculous statements as supreme wisdom. Use their curveballs as proof that they are an idiot savant who understands the subject in ways the human brain cannot yet comprehend.

ENSEMBLE PLAY

A good team allows each other to play the entire spectrum of human nature without apology. A great teammate gives you permission to be dangerous, ugly, daring, quiet, profound, pretentious, and reactionary. Whether you're playing an angel or a monster, their support is unconditional and unwavering.

Trust is built through actions and it takes honest discussions and a shared aesthetic and mission. Communication and agreement are how players show love and build fearlessness. Only then can they unlock their brilliance and explore the depths and heights of humanity.

Great teams have a gift for mischief and knowing when it's needed. They can make an audience care about nonsense. They make choices, not excuses. They take risks, make discoveries together, and cheer and champion each other's genius. They're fearless and vulnerable, pouring everything, their entire selves into the work to make something greater.

It takes years of training for an ensemble to anticipate each other's moves, to glide smoothly through a scene with telepathy.

Newer improvisers want to be this smooth, but it takes work, repetition and trust to roll with each other. Stubborn players are unbending, unwilling to step off course. Everything needs to be just so. When the improv connection isn't there, impatient players get frustrated with their partner for not seeing what the scene was meant to be and they hit their thighs to express this. *I know this is bad. Don't you see how frustrated I am up here with this person? Don't think that I think that this is good. I know this is bad. That's why I'm hitting my legs. Because I don't want you to think I have bad taste or that this is how the scene was supposed to go.*

This sells out the scene. Note this right away. Hitting their thighs will not resuscitate the scene. It only induces more panic and telegraphs how bad it is and how judgmental they are. An improviser must learn to stay in a state of flow to maintain momentum and course correct without pouting or stopping.

To illustrate this, mime that you are pushing against a giant boulder in the center of the room. It doesn't budge. Take a different angle, strain and struggle, and show the sweat. Finally, it lifts and rocks to a side. It's not perfectly round so every corner and edge makes it clumsy. Show how it tumbles, klutzy, not always by your control. *Careful, clear out of the way!* Explain that you'd like to give it to someone in the room, but as you go that way, the boulder veers to the left. Stop and pout about it. Now you have to strain and struggle again just to get it moving.

You can't always control the speed, finesse and direction of a scene. If a scene is moving generally in the right direction, keep it moving. Its momentum makes it easier to steer, and adjust to move smoothly through the room.

The more comfortable we are with being imperfect, the more we can move through those moments without wasting all the heavy lifting and brain power and exhaustion of constantly stopping a scene dead in its tracks just because it's off by a hair.

TAG TEAM SCENES

Begin by inviting two players to start a scene. After twenty seconds pause the scene. Ask the group to comb through it, calling out character traits they identified. Were characters greedy or giving, chaotic or calculated? Let the group discuss their observations. This helps players hear and see their first moves by spotlighting them.

Performers can be humbled to hear their choices are not ringing through to the audience as they intended.

DEFENSIVE STUDENT: *Well, that's what I was going to do, but I didn't get there yet.*

Note this defensiveness right away. This is not about what they planned to do. This is about what they have done and how audiences interpreted those choices. Players must acknowledge and adjust to better radiate their choices with fidelity.

Drill these. Encourage players to be intentional, starting scenes with attitudes, opinions, status, spine and idiosyncrasies.

Now limit it to ten seconds, then to five.

Players may balk that there's not enough time to establish anything. How they carry themselves, look at each other, interact, and how close or far away they are gives the audience particulars which they use to construct meaning. However, most improvisers are so in their heads that these choices go unnoticed. They are so busy searching for a big idea, that they miss the little things, the seeds of the scene they've already found. Shine a light on these to help them bloom into rich character games.

Invite the audience to study the characters; when they see something, they will hop up and tag into the scene and continue as the character, following the fun and accentuating their nature. The tag acts as a laser pointer highlighting a single aspect or quirk and follows its logic through the scene.

This can be revelatory. Players realize all they need to do is listen to themselves and pattern what is already there. The first move is enough. It's everything. When improvisers second guess their choices or invent new ones, the scene snakes off track instead of finding a clear path.

Encourage the players to tag in and out, like wrestlers, so there's a constant sense of heightening to the scene.

Channeling a character outside our own wheelhouse is liberating. It awakens new choices and logic. Improvisers get stuck in their ways and ruts. If an initiation works, it gets folded into the rotation and if it doesn't, it gets scrapped forever. Improvisers get trapped in these paths and can't surprise themselves anymore. We're so desperate to get on base that we stop swinging for the fences. Without the onus of the initiation being *ours*, it allows players to be more adventurous.

Next, invite the entire backline to share and channel a single character. This can get crazy quickly. Remind players that the scene matters more than the exercise. If a tsunami of tags destroys any semblance of a scene, then all that energy and inventiveness are lost.

Challenge the ensemble to use their collective imagination to tag and heighten the scene beyond their perceived ceilings. Then call scene. Immediately have the same two players start again with the same lines. This time the entire backline will tag the other character, mining their nature for fun. This exercise proves any choice can be heightened and spurs players to work as an ensemble to reach new heights.

SNOW WHITE SCENES

Too many group games begin with *Everybody get in here*. Then everyone rushes to label themselves with an obnoxious trait as a placeholder for their character, *the kiss ass, the brainiac, the cool dude*, and *the rude one*. This is not a scene, it's a cast list of characters for a very bad play. There is no room to pattern behavior because everyone is too busy saying who they are, telling instead of showing, listing instead of playing a relationship.

Improv schools stress that players gift themselves with a deal. It's an essential skill. However, some players miss the meaning. They gift themselves with a name tag but never play the behavior. They stand there on stage a listed, whisper of a personality. It's as if they give themselves this gift not to play it but to tick a box and appease the teacher by naming themselves. *But I had a game! I said it when I came in. I said I'm the cranky type.* They are more concerned with bracing for the notes they'll get after the show than the fun they could have during it.

This is a casualty of art being institutionalized. Where notes and rubrics outweigh the craft and upstage impulses, teachers must call this out. Don't let players give themselves empty gifts and get away with it. Don't reward hollow characters. Help them embody and inspirit their choices. Strong points of view give scenes traction.

Co-sign dumb ideas with every ounce of your brain.

The proportionality of a two-person scene does not correspond one-to-one with a group scene. A two-person scene has time and room to establish character games while also building a relationship. Group scenes don't. They need recalibration or everyone fights the first half of the scene to be heard, piling their *deals* on top of other players' *deals*, building a wobbly, precarious Jenga tower of a scene that buckles and topples the fun.

When the stage feels crowded and the audience feels confused, note it. No matter how many people are on stage, two-minute scenes only need two points of view. Think Snow White and the Seven Dwarfs. It's not Snow White and Happy and Sneezy and Sleepy and Doc, Grumpy and Dopey, and Bashful. It's the one and the many.

In the first minute of a scene, players must establish how the one feels about the many, and how the many feel about the one. Snow White is grateful to the dwarfs, and the dwarfs are smitten with Snow White. They dance and parade around her as their may-pole. Once this relationship is set through repetition, the characters can discover nuances that individualize themselves.

Begin this drill with eight on the backline. Have a player step forward and perform a non-verbal task, such as a farmer throwing grain to the ground.

Now invite a player from the backline to make a choice that directly relates to the farmer. They enter clucking like a chicken and pecking at the grain.

The farmer will continue to throw grain, and the chicken will continue to peck at it. Now invite a third to join, mirroring one of the two choices. Their choice will cinch the dynamic.

If they join clucking, the rest of the backline will also enter as chickens grazing at the shins of the lone farmer.

If they enter throwing grain, the rest will enter as farmers spoiling a single chicken with grain, until it is fat and fed.

This technique simplifies the scene, distilling the relationship by maintaining two points of view. Keep it simple.

A player enters, as a restaurant manager, clapping.

> MANAGER: *Can we get the staff out here? Where is everyone?*

One by one the waiters, kitchen staff and hosts enter, tired and sluggish. The manager is infuriated by their dawdling.

The restaurant manager may have had another idea when they initiated but the behavior is already so fun that the scene doesn't need their idea. Hopefully, the player has the savvy to make the staff's behavior the reason they were calling the meeting.

> MANAGER: *Hurry up! I'm gonna wait for everyone to get in here because this is important. Everyone needs to hear this.*

Now each player can milk it, arriving more tired than the next. At one point, the last employee enters then everybody turns on a dime yelling, *Why are you always late?!* The two warring sides banding together to lash out at a single waiter is unexpected; it inverts the game from the one against many to the many against one.

It's ridiculous how something so simple and dumb can be so playful and satisfying. Improvisers obsess and dedicate so much time to discussing improv theory and sharpening skills but at its simplest, it's obvious dumb fun that is patterned and played as a group. This type of group game scene work is vital to any improv curriculum.

TOY CHEST

Begin by dragging a large improvised toy chest into the middle of the room. Show that it has heft. Ask someone to grab the other end. Set it down, thumb its latches, and flip open the trunk. Explain that inside is every toy or object imaginable. Pull out three balls and begin juggling them. Use your eyes to track the balls in space, then trace them as they fall back into the trunk.

Now invite anyone to pull out a toy and begin playing with it. Whether it is a kite, a Tomogatchi egg, one of those old-school Water Arcades, or an RC Drone, it is the player's job to love playing with their object and ping off it to find out more about themself. If it's a set of watercolors, maybe they see art in everything and take pride in every brushstroke. If it's a remote control car, maybe the player realizes they're an adrenaline junkie that lives fast and reckless.

It's important players know how they feel about their object as they play and interact with it. They are responsible for heightening How they feel about What they've chosen.

Once this bond is established, invite the rest to declare how they feel about the person playing with the toy. Whatever attitude is expressed first is embraced by the whole ensemble. Their goal is to heighten by reinforcing each other's offers.

> DON: *Look at him with that RC Car! He's a little daredevil.*
> JILL: *Mmhm he is. I'd say more devil than dare.*
> CHARLIE: *He's a little hellion. Janice has her hands full.*
> LAURA: *Oh, I know, the daycares won't take him anymore.*
> KELLY: *Nope, they say he's Satan himself.*

Some players hide in the crowd, unengaged. Call it out. Encourage them to comment, be an active listener, to make whatever is in play matter. The collective goal is to heighten by reinforcing each other's offers.

As long as the child commits to the toy and the ensemble heightens their observations of the child, the scene will grow. When the scene builds to an emphatic end, the player places their toy back into the box and another can grab a new object.

New improvisers tend to make the same choices, either loving or hating the player and their toy. This gets stale. Have players give themselves an adjective as a lens to put an edge on their choices. Get irked, or be skeptical, concerned, condescending, close-minded, nostalgic, sincere, humbled, demure, delighted, bored, squeamish, militant or haughty and pretentious. Defined attitudes and attributes are rocket fuel for characterization. It gives their POV teeth.

Now when someone begins painting with their watercolors, the observer can be in awe of their genius.

> JILL: *Isn't that beautiful.*

DON: *She's gifted.*
MAX: *She's a genius.*
LAURA: *She's ahead of her time.*
MAX: *I'm speechless.*
JILL: *Me too. I feel stupid.*
DON: *I know it's saying something profound but I don't understand it.*

Or cutting and unkind.

MAX: *Oh, this is going to be a mess.*
JILL: *We should have done this outside.*
DON: *She thinks she's Jackson Pollock.*
LAURA: *Even he knew he needed to get some of it on the canvas.*

There's an infinite number of gifts a player can give themself, so don't choose to play an idea you don't like. Imagine a child on a playground sulking with a Slinky, in tears and ashamed of it. No one wants to play with that kid. When players breathe life and detail into their offers, it's magnetic. People are drawn to them and want to join in on their fun. The same is true for any initiation. Players must love their choices. That's not to say that players have to love everyone and every object in every scene all the time. Improvisers show love by playing, exploring, growing ideas and having and heightening their opinions.

Now, invite them to pull things from the trunk that aren't toys: a pet pig, a bulldozer, a topiary, a crossbow or flame retardant stunt man goo.

Nadia crosses to the trunk and pulls out a pack of cigarettes.

Have her play with it, ping off it, have opinions about it, and grow it so that it has its own gravitational pull that attracts others to want to play with her toys or build off her fun.

She hits the pack against her hand, then pulls out a cigarette, trying to be tough. Their friends chime in, concerned.

EVA: *What are you doing? You don't smoke cigarettes.*
AMANDA: *You don't know whose those are.*
CASEY: *Yeah, they could be some psycho's.*

Nadia puts the cigarette in her mouth.

> EVA: *Wait, they could be laced with something.*
> AMANDA: *Yeah, and you're not even old enough.*

Nadia lights the cigarette and inhales.

> CASEY: *Uh, hello, cancer?!*

The friends flip out, distressed and sickened by every drag the player takes.

Next, invite a concerned friend, Eva, to interact with the object directly. When she touches the cigarette, she will shed her concern and feel the same spell cast on her to take a drag. She does and her friends scream even louder.

> AMANDA: *What are you doing? You were supposed to put it out!*
> CASEY: *Did you forget what you were just saying!*

Eva takes a drag, then blows the smoke into Nadia's mouth.

> CASEY: *Peer pressure is no joke!*
> AMANDA: *You're going to kill us all!*

Amanda grabs the cigarette out Evas' mouth and shoos away the smoke. As Amanda holds it, smoke catches in her nostrils, and the same spell overcomes her. At this point the playfulness is unhinged. The three smoke like chimneys, becoming more and more incorrigible and rude as Casey prays for their souls.

VINES

Dynamic edits move from one scene to the next on a dime. They use eye contact to trigger preloaded scenes to start in the middle with momentum and emotional torque.

Begin with six players up. As they mill about, they establish a unique, non-verbal interaction with each of the other five performers. There should always be at least two if not three *scene starts* happening simultaneously.

Amy and Beau lock eyes. Amy drops to a knee genuflecting to Beau. Beau fields the choice by drawing a sword and knighting Amy. Bound to this exchange, any time Amy and Beau lock eyes again, she will drop to a knee and Beau will knight her.

The players find new partners. Amy connects with Kai and Beau connects with Chet.

Kai draws a switchblade, pointing it at Amy. Amy surrenders with her hands in the air. Meanwhile, Beau wistfully hugs Chet. Chet squirms but Beau hugs them closer.

It shouldn't take more than two minutes for the fifteen different scene initiations to be hammered out.

Now invite players to move around. If they meet eyes with someone, they swing to revisit their dynamic, then swing to another. Players are not speaking or forwarding these scenes narratively. They are simply adding emotional weight and realism to these loaded dynamics, hungry to move and reconnect with as many players as possible until the room is abuzz.

Through repetition these scenes are revved, ready. Eye contact is the only spark players need to burst into the next scene.

Next, have the six players form a backline for a fifteen-minute montage. Instead of sweep edits, they will use eye contact to land in their preloaded dynamic using the stage picture and tension as a springboard to speak in their scene. Amy and Kai lock eyes and Kai pulls a switchblade and Amy begins to tremble.

> KAI: *Give me your watch!*
> AMY: *Here, take it!*
> KAI: *Wait, this an Apple watch!*
> AMY: *Yeah, it's a series 9.*
> KAI: *Forget it. I have a PC.*
> AMY: *Whatever you want! Just don't hurt me.*
> KAI: *Fine, give me your wallet!*
> AMY: *Here!!*
> KAI: *This is a phone.*
> AMY: *Yeah, I use Apple Wallet. It's an app on my iPhone! Please don't kill me!*

Amy begs, pleading with Kai to spare her life.

To edit, Beau comes off the backline and catches the eyes of Amy on their knees. Instantly, they shift. Amy's sniveling becomes a prideful oath. Beau with authority and grandeur commences with Amy's knighting ceremony, as Kai vanishes to the backline.

Sharp edits cut the fat to start on action. This brings energy and momentum to every scene throughout the piece.

Newer improvisers will cut good scenes short, rushing to get to their idea. Note it right away. Creating a scene is the hardest part. Once it's up and running, get as much play out of it before swinging to a new one.

As ensembles get more adept at this technique, set a rule that a scene cannot swing to a new scene until it has escalated enough, the way the DeLorean in *Back to the Future* cannot time travel unless it reaches 88 miles per hour and has 1.21 gigawatts of power. Once a scene has heightened from solid to liquid to gas, then and only then can eye contact launch a new scene.

Still, advise players to avoid meaningful eye contact. Hungry eyes feel like they are baiting a new scene.

Don't be desperate for the future.

Play the present scene, keep the focus where it belongs and when the edit is there, take it with your eyes like launching a nuclear missile to swing to the next scene together.

Example: Chet nuzzles his cheek against the shin of Leo and Leo pets Chet like a cat. When this dynamic is reprised in the montage, the whole backline supports as cats, flooding in from every door, cupboard, closet, cushion and window. The man and his house full of cats is an active game. He can name the cats, feed them, show the audience their tricks and give them treats. When the edit is there, a cat makes meaningful eye contact with Beau and lands in his arms with deliberateness. Instantly, Chet tries wriggling out of Beau's embrace.

CHET: *It's hard to say goodbye when you won't let me leave.*

These scenes leap off the stage. They are arresting and effortless because they are birthed from action and reaction as opposed to discussing a scene into existence. Here players know their dynamic, reinvest in the action of it, and enunciate the emotion and when they can speak, words are simply used to give more dimension to what is already being played.

MAKE THE ORDINARY EXTRAORDINARY

An ensemble works together to make every scene as great as it can be. Sometimes that involves giving teammates space to grow a scene, cradling with environment, tagging to a new location to place the scene in a context that complements the game, or making a quick walk-on to add clarity for the players or the audience. Every member must be engaged and dedicated to making every choice extraordinary.

Begin with six players on a backline. Invite one to initiate an ordinary activity.

Patrick sits center stage, crosses his legs, and begins to meditate. He breathes in and out.

It is the ensemble's job to make that activity extraordinary.

Ella on the backline offers noise, and obnoxious yelling.

Patrick, meditating, prickles then adjusts and continues to breathe.

The backline patterns the first choice creating more noise: cars honk, bells ring, text messages ding, and jackhammers rumble.

Patrick squares his shoulders and takes a big breath in, and the entire backline is reduced to a whisper. Patrick's spine elongates. From the backline Clay holds a high-pitched *Tingggg* of enlightenment and the rest of the backline helps to hold the note longer than humanly possible. Patrick is in a state of bliss as he breathes.

Off the backline Ari rushes in undulating as Patrick's aura, and others join, increasing its power and reach. Another, Mila, offers warm fuzzy memories from the meditator's past and others celebrate it, offering more. This strokes the character's ego, but they adjust their shoulders and breathe, pushing past this, and the compliments fade to a whisper, and their aura surges, growing even more powerful.

Everyone begins to hum.

The backline transforms the meditator into a queen, another player becomes their throne, and another feeds them grapes. With each breath the backline transforms into another alternate reality, unfurling, one more spectacular than the next. The backline works to levitate a chair, and then all chairs in the room lift off the floor and move in concert orbiting the character deep in meditation.

In an instant, all furniture lands on the ground, and the entire backline lifts Patrick high off the ground, then sets them down where they started, the compliments return, the ting repeats, and slowly the whisper of city noise fills the room and Patrick opens their eyes.

Group ownership makes this possible. Without it, the scene is a single person sitting centerstage breathing with their eyes closed. A very brave but very boring move.

Underline the unsung support moves that help scenes take flight. When these selfless, unglamorous moves are acknowledged in notes, it puts a premium on championing each other. This gives value to how an idea is fortified. This shifts the paradigm; the base blocks of the human pyramid become just as important as the player on top. Ideas and how they are fielded are equally valued. The seed needs the soil as much as the soil needs the seed.

This evolution awakens trust in the ensemble. They can be daring, jump into the unknown, run out with half an idea, and know the team will catch them.

Fifty percent confidence, fifty percent connectivity and a dash of funny, or drama, or absurdism: that's the recipe. This may oversimplify improv but most notes come down to this proportion being off. Some players try to overcompensate for a lack of connectivity with more confidence. This is like not having water for a pie crust so they put in more flour.

Until players have this ratio down for themselves, it can be difficult to trust others. Attempts at ensemble work feel hollow, like a team of lone wolf mercenaries out for their own glory. The connectivity is only there because it's assigned, not because it's felt or valued. So the confidence and trust wobble. When the scene shakes, it sends players to their panic moves to survive the scene, selling out their teammates.

This exercise exposes a team for what it is. It shows players' weaknesses, fears, and desire for self-preservation and glory.

Every class is different. Not every team is an ensemble. Not every player plays well in groups. Not everyone is ready to risk at the same time. But pushing this type of work to the later levels of an improv curriculum risks never developing this muscle at all.

An ensemble is selfless; it spotlights the genius of its individuals. Help teams breathe and push past their ego and the noise and glory to make something extraordinary with each other.

EDITING

The majority of an improv curriculum focuses on scene work, the bones of a piece. How scenes fit together and move from one to the next is often an afterthought.

When a scene reaches its height, it needs an edit. A player from the backline runs across the front of the stage wiping the previous scene away and returning to the backline. This is a standard sweep edit. It clears the stage, tabula rasa, giving players of the next scene a blank canvas to initiate. It's clean and utilitarian as a visual cue for the audience but best reserved when everyone on stage has been slaughtered, or the stage picture reaches Where's Waldo level chaos. In these cases, it provides an audience a chance to stop laughing and catch their breath.

> **Note:** Not every scene warrants a reset of this magnitude. Sweeping a sputtering scene can be deadly. An unearned sweep edit leaves a big silence in its wake. The show comes to a screeching halt: it shakes the ensemble's confidence and gives the audience too much time to judge what they just saw.

An edit is a punctuation mark. And a sweep edit is an exclamation point! No one likes when people use too many exclamation points!! It makes them seem ordinary! And now they need to use two or three of them to even get their point across!!!

Edits can be so much more. They offer an opportunity to infuse the piece with motifs, themes and commentary.

If the suggestion is *Luck*, a backline player may shout, *Red 19. No winners. No winners!* as the ensemble forms a roulette chip rake clearing the previous characters from the stage.

A backline player may yell, ***All bets in! Let's spin that wheel!*** The ensemble skips out forming a ring around the scene. A new player stands in the center of the circle, closes their eyes and points in front of them. The members spinning on the outside slowly come to a stop, striking bold character stances. Whomever the center player is pointing at starts a scene with their character and all other players return to the backline.

Perhaps later in the piece, when luck isn't so rosy and characters have gambled their lives away, a backline player may enter and shout, ***Re-Po Man!*** and then lift players up mid-sentence, clearing them off, repossessing the chairs, the audience, the lights, taking everything they can from the scene.

These edits truly embrace the spirit of luck and create commentary about the highs and lows of gambling.

Transitions are ligaments that connect the bones of our piece.

Drill these dynamic transitions by having players perform a ten-minute montage that prioritizes edits over scene work. Insist that no scene be longer than thirty seconds. To get started, provide players with an overarching theme as a suggestion, such as Cinema, Metamorphosis, Dance, Ethics, Magic, Military, Artificial Intelligence, etc. After each piece, note what worked, and stress clarity and inventiveness, repetition and reinvestment.

A plane burns most of its fuel on its takeoff. Once a show starts, players should use its momentum like a Rube Goldberg machine to kick out and transfer the energy of one scene and fold it into the next.

Splitting the stage in latitudes is helpful. It allows where players stand to signal how they intend to support the scene. The stage is split in three: upstage, centerstage, and downstage. Most scenes take place centerstage. If a player would like to create atmosphere in the background, they should exist upstage of the scene and be a little muted. If a background character steps forward joining the characters centerstage, this signifies a walk-on. If a player crosses just a little further downstage of the main characters, this communicates that they would like to take the focus in the scene. If they cross all the way downstage without eye contact, obliterating any established furniture, it is safe to presume this player is editing the existing scene and starting something new.

A punch-through edit offers a jolt of energy into the next scene. When a player on the backline wants to edit the existing scene, they simply step through the scene, splitting the characters like saloon doors and initiating. This cues players in the previous scene to peel off and join the backline. This punch-through is arresting. It immediately gives the audience something new to track and zero time to judge or assess the last scene.

Encourage players to use a punch-through edit with a line in hand. This cuts any room for silence or misinterpretation and immediately platforms the next scene with energy.

For more sophistication, invite players to use a punch-through with *Last line-First line*, where they grab the very last thing said on stage and repeat it with a different tone to create a new context. The repetition clues the ensemble and the audience that this is a new scene. This technique invites a level of danger into the piece, as there's no room to craft an initiation. Instead, players are taking the focus not because they have an idea but because it's time for one. This is a selfless edit that honors tempo and pacing over inspiration.

Another type of edit extracts an object from a pre-existing scene to use it in a different context for a new scene. If two parents are assembling gift bags and party favors for a child's birthday, a player on the backline may storm downstage, snagging a party bag out of a parent's hand and vomiting into it, transforming the scene from a suburban kitchen to a 747. A flight attendant approaches them, **Sir, you need to sit down. The plane is about to take off.**

As another option, the player can extract an object and then morph it into something new. The vomiting man sits as the plane taxis on the tarmac. His wife tries to comfort him, but he's embarrassed. She kisses his wedding ring and says, ***I married you because I love how sensitive you are.*** A player crosses off the backline, pulls the wedding ring off the player's finger, stretches it into a tiara and places it on her head to become a young princess or stretches it even further to become a hula hoop.

This technique offers more sophistication and control. Instead of just a pull-and-play, it allows the initiator from the backline to pluck something from the reality of the previous scene and transform it into something more in alignment with a premise they were planning.

RECYCLE, REUSE, REPURPOSE

The instructor begins on stage carefully tying their shoes using the phrase, *Over, under, around and through, meet Mr.Bunny, pull and through.*

Then the instructor asks the class what they observed.

> STUDENT 1: *You tied your shoes.*

Invite them to be specific. What exactly happened? How did it happen?

> STUDENT 2: *You tied your shoes like a child and said a phrase to help you remember.*

The instructor repeats the activity, *Over, under, around and through, meet Mr.Bunny, pull and through.*

Now invite a volunteer to recreate exactly what they saw, followed by another and another. Much like Cooey Cooey Cooey, the mundane task is elevated through repetition to something dynamic and watchable.

Next invite players to repurpose the phrase in new scenarios.

> A player uses the phrase as they mime tightening a duchess's corset.
> Another uses the phrase as they tie shut a pillowcase full of kittens.
> Another ties a tourniquet around their arm before shooting heroin.
> Another ties a bow around a box of cannolis.

Exhaust the phrase until there are no other ideas. Then push the players to keep going. This instills confidence that the single little phrase they have is enough.

> Another teaches a kid how to tie a tie for the first time.
> Another ties a blindfold and then throws knives at a target.
> Another delivers a baby and ties the umbilical cord.
> Another ties a noose around their neck.

Players don't need to constantly invent new things. There's a certain point in every piece where it's enough to just invest in what has been created. Players can recycle and repurpose information and specifics in new ways to keep it fresh and surprising. Even when the audience knows it's coming, they delight in the repetition of it all.

Repetition and reinvestment help a piece cohere. It's Chekhov's principle: if a gun is introduced in act one, it should go off in act three. Every element in a story should be necessary. Anything irrelevant should be removed.

It's a gift to be able to list, invent and create. Not everyone has that gift. Run wild with it. Load the first third of a piece with specifics, striking imagery, unforgettable characters and fierce opinions. That's all the information that's needed for the entire set. Use the next two-thirds to reinvest, braid what you've made, and weave it together to become the fabric of the piece. This gives the set a scripted theatrical feel.

Not all players have the ability to hear what they've created or if it's worthy of being patterned. Their gift is their curse. They zig-zag and *AND*, going on Robin Williams-es-que free-associative rants. Their ability to reinvest is underdeveloped because it's easier for them to create something new than identify and invest in what they've made.

On the other end of the spectrum, players may be incapable of coming up with information but are brilliant at weaving it together, folding in details, discerning, recalling, and repurposing.

A great improviser can do both. A great ensemble has a sense of when it is time to seed and grow and when it is time to harvest and reprise. Without this shared sense, pieces become overstuffed, inelegant, and shapeless like a pillowcase shoved full of meowing kittens drowning at the bottom of our own stream of consciousness.

Reinvestment dazzles. It pickles the piece in its own brine. Be hungry to highlight, reprise and call each other's gifts back in the exact right way at the exact right time to elevate a piece to new heights.

PIVOT EDITS

Begin with two players on stage. Their objective is to perform two scenes with seamless edits that hinge from one reality to another and back.

> **Zack receives the suggestion: Vandalism**
> **Luke receives the suggestion: College**

Zack is invited to begin a scene honoring their suggestion. Luke is tasked with finding an edit in the first scene that will allow them to hinge seamlessly into a second scene honoring their suggestion.

Zack initiates as a police officer arresting a vandal for graffiti. Luke takes the gifts and becomes belligerent, full of piss and vinegar yelling at the officer as he handcuffs him against the cop car.

The first scene will find its own game, its own rules and a set of characters. They will play this until it reaches a high point.

The cop struggles to get the vandal under control and tries pushing him into the back-seat of the police vehicle. The vandal spits, calling the cop every name in the book. The cop finally muscles the vandal into the car. As soon as Luke lands in the backseat, they pivot to a new scene honoring *college*.

Luke's eyes shift from wiry to optimistic and full of promise. He looks at Zack.

LUKE: *Mom, look, Cornell and it's a thick envelope. That's got to be good news, right?*

Instantly, Zack drops his cop demeanor and takes on the spine of a chipper and sup-portive mother. Luke opens the letter but the hope in his face washes away as he reads it. The mom tries to get her child's spirits up as she presents the next envelope. They both say a little prayer over it before they open it to find that it's another rejection. Luke hands a third envelope to his mom. The mom kisses her son on the forehead and then looks down to open the letter. Zack pulls the letter from the envelope and pivots, reading Miranda Rights to the vandal as the cop.

As an added challenge, invite players to weave language from one scene into the other and vice versa. This creates a latticework between worlds, binding the scenes and elevating them.

The skill to braid and juggle multiple games with breakneck pivots is thrilling.

If players are not fully present and dropped into their choices, these pivots will be lost. Pivot edits demand connectivity and decisiveness. Scenes must have disparate heat signatures, tone, and sense of humor. One scene may be earnest, the other slapstick, another grounded or fantastical — contrast helps scene partners and audiences detect these pivots. Push players to play characters outside themselves. If they refuse, it will be tough to identify character shifts at all.

Players must look for a loaded moment so that the pivot is sharp, whether that be through eye contact, meaningful touch, an empty stage, an exit or through object work.

Eye Contact — Connectivity is essential. Players must channel their characters and radiate their souls through their eyes to their scene partners. When a scene crests players will often look away from each other to break the tension. This is a perfect opportunity to pivot. When players catch each other's eyes again, invite them to do so with a new spirit, channeling a new character, and insist they speak to this energy instantly, through a new voice and spine so that there is no room for misinterpretation.

Meaningful Touch — Whether it's a hug, a pat on the shoulder, or a squeeze of the hand, physical actions yield reactions, and that's a perfect time to pivot. Imagine a competitive coach trying to get an ADHD little leaguer to focus before they take the plate. They grab the child by the shoulders and shake them, then at once the energy shifts to lustful lovers embracing, saying their goodbyes before one boards the Titanic.

Empty Stage — In the rare event that an improv stage is left empty, use it. Imagine both players amid a museum heist after hours; they cartwheel between lasers, somersault to avoid cameras, duck off stage at the sound of a security guard, then they return to stage as two self-conscious widows entering a salsa class for the first time.

Exits and Entrances — When a character exits a scene, it draws the audience's focus to the door; use that focus to pivot on the door closing and then instantly opening to a new scene. Imagine two neighbors sitting at a kitchen table. One gives the other a lighthouse ornament for having watched their house while they were on vacation in Cape Cod, then their air fryer dings and they excuse themselves. When the player returns, they burst through the door like a battering ram as a paramedic on the graveyard shift pushing a gurney and shouting to the ER nurse for help.

Objects — A prison guard slides a plate of food to a convict. The convict kicks it back under the door, the prison guard shoves it back. Every time they shuttle the plate back and forth it gets more important. As players interact with an object it becomes this white-hot focal point. The audience starts to visualize the plate as it's kicked and shoved. It becomes real. Their collective imagination makes it real. Now is the moment to grab the plate and transform it, skip it as a rock across a peaceful pond and watch it skim across the water into the next father and son scene.

CHARACTER & CONTEXT

Prompt a player to become a squirrel and stationary players to become trees. Challenge the ensemble to take group ownership of the squirrel as it scurries around the woods. As the squirrel darts up a tree, that tree becomes the squirrel and the squirrel replaces the tree. This allows the audience to trace the darting path of the squirrel with their eyes from downstage left to upstage right before a new player as the squirrel barrels down-stage right to another tree. This demands engagement. Players are either the scenery or they are the focus. They are the Interesting or the Interested. Players must understand this ebb and flow, and the need for engagement and clarity.

Now add to the exercise. Invite a player to move as a new character. Push them to always be in a state of being or becoming, refining every movement, distilling their emotions, and sharpening their worldview. The others remain stationary but alert, antennas up, listening to understand.

A mover may hobble with a cane Ebeneezer Scrooge-like. It is their job to honor their first choice and continue to grow it.

Note: This does not mean be louder. It invites exploration, discovery and rein-vestment. They will *bah humbug*, sneer and scowl. Adding detail, nuance, and importance to their idea. They are building momentum while they forge the character's line of logic.

Empower the stationary players to celebrate the mover by surrounding them with environmental elements creating a backdrop that envelops the mover, as the trees cradled the squirrel.

As Ebeneezer stomps past, they can wave and wish him a Merry Christmas from their rooted position. Another may offer cranberry corn pudding, at which he scoffs. Another asks for a donation to the orphanage.

EBENEEZER: *Humbug!*

These offers create context for the mover. They are kindling to burn the mover's character choices brighter. As Ebeneezer pushes past people, it builds theatricality, simulating the bustling chaos of a Dickensian city as they dart through the streets of London.

The ensemble works together to create an illusion that elevates beyond normal physics to make something magical.

When the scene crests, immediately invite a new person to move with a new idea.

Think of it as a phoenix; each idea builds from an ember to a flame, to a fire, to a blaze, and is eventually reduced to ash revealing a new ember for another idea to grow. Underline this lifecycle when it happens organically. Only in these fiery, gaseous states should players initiate a new idea. This rule allows players to move without worry of it being seen as an invading initiation. Now they can support and fan the flames of an ember to grow the fun of the scene to a blaze.

The more they repeat this exercise, the less it will need to be directed from the outside. Help the ensemble to grow ideas into an inferno and find that sweet spot to pivot to a new dynamic with a new mover, a new context that has its own dynamic, tempo and game.

Encourage selfless support and undeniably sharp initiations. Train the ensemble to look for white-hot moments in their scenes when the game burns its brightest. That is when a new scene should erupt from the old. Use the focus in your favor, wherever the action is, wherever the audience's eye is, pivot there and punch through.

> **Note:** In some instances, it makes sense to share the role of the squirrel. In others, it doesn't. If they're sharing the mover role within the first thirty seconds, then that will likely continue. If they don't share the mover's role, there's a good chance they will stick to their initial roles.

Of course, there are no hard rules. If the mover is a mad scientist experimenting with chemicals, it might make narrative sense, two minutes in, when they take a swig of it, that they become another person or beast altogether.

FLOCKING

Flocking is a hybrid of a Slow Burn Matching scene, coupled with a carousel, where players inhabit a single space with various points of view with immediate connectivity.

The mechanics begin with a four-person scene where players are cut from the same cloth.

A player rushes in on an office chair, pointing at a spot downstage.

> JACKIE: *Just sign in there. Just sign in there on the clipboard, and we'll call you. Mmhm.*

Three other players roll into the scene, matching and pointing.

> NOLAN: *Just sign in! And the doctor will see you soon.*
> LARA: *There's a clipboard. It's right there.*
> ARLEN: *Just put your John Hancock down, mmhm*
> JACKIE: *But print it, please.*
> LARA: *Neatly, so we can read it.*
> NOLAN: *The doctor needs to know who he's seeing!*

These receptionists all roll their eyes at the ghosted character, then return to bobbing in their chairs. They whisper and gossip, and every once in a while are interrupted by patients whom they all gang up on.

When the scene has defined characters and a pronounced game, one player peels off from the group to re-enter the scene as a new supplemental character. In this example, it makes sense to populate as a patient approaching the receptionists. (That's not to say that choice is the best; it could be anyone or anything: a doctor; a delivery person; a mouse; a bizarre representation of the receptionists' biggest regrets, etc.)

It's important to act swiftly. Lara dips upstage of the matching scene, takes a new position on stage and re-enters with confidence, addressing the receptionists:

> LARA: *Hi, I'm Mitchell. I'm here for a 12:15 with Doctor Katzel.*
> NOLAN: *Just sign in there. There's a clipboard.*
> JACKIE: *It's clear as day.*
> ARLEN: *Mmhm!*
> JACKIE: *We'll call you. Just sign in.*
> LARA: *Well the thing is, is I'm a little early but …*
> JACKIE: *Just sign in.*
> ARLEN: *Nice and neat. So we can read it.*
> NOLAN: *No big autographs.*

This three-to-one dynamic plays like a Snow White scene. As the relationship between these two points of view becomes clear, another receptionist will dip away to join as another patient.

> NOLAN: *Hi, I'm Lawrence again. I've been waiting for more than an hour.*
> JACKIE: *Just sign in there and we'll call your name.*
> NOLAN: *I did …*
> ARLEN: *We've got a system.*
> NOLAN: *It's just I've been waiting for quite some time.*
> JACKIE: *Well, we're running a little behind.*
> ARLEN: *Because people like you are constantly stopping us from doing our job.*
> JACKIE: *… to explain how a sign-in sheet works. It gums up the gears.*
> ARLEN: *It's like giving a dog a Rice Krispie treat.*
> JACKIE: *Is that bad for dogs?*
> ARLEN: *Oh, yes, it gums up my Millie-girl real bad.*

Steadily the majority becomes the minority. Four-person scenes become three-to-one scenes, then two-to-two then one-to-three until eventually all four players have adopted the new point of view on the other side of the waiting room.

The mechanics are similar to a grade school Caboose Run, where a group jogs in a straight line and the last runner must sprint to the front of the jogging line. This continues until everyone has sprinted from caboose to engine, at which point the group is reborn, in this case from receptionists to patients. Now players can sit in the waiting room and build the energy and game of these helpless patients in need of medical attention until one player peels off from the group to re-enter the scene as a new supplemental character, possibly a doctor.

Flocking requires connectivity and demands that players stay engaged, while in their brains, they zoom out to gain a bird's eye view to identify what the piece needs or might be lacking. Players must be both character and writer/director.

This technique allows ensembles to create atmosphere, be objects, be abstract, or avant-garde. They can bend space and reveal story in a patient and masterful way with tons of agreement. At any point, they can stop peeling and dig on the fun of those one-against-many scenes or going two against two or relishing in all four being the same again. All these variations, permutations and mirroring can have an almost kaleidoscopic feel. With expertise, these techniques can be used to make dynamic scenography that elevates the matching scene to something truly theatrical.

A player initiates crossing downstage, turning their back to the audience and stretching their arms gnarled above their head like tree branches. Another player plants themselves further upstage, and another.

The initial player begins hooting like an owl. They hold on this woodsy tableau. The crack of branches and the chirp of crickets create an atmosphere that draws the audience in. Player A *YES, AND*s this. They throw their voice.

JOVAN: *It's over here!*

The audience hears the rustle of leaves. Jovan spins around, miming that they just came from behind the tree they were inhabiting. They carry a cooler and yell upstage over their shoulder.

> JOVAN: *Oh, man, this place is rad!*

Jovan interacts with their surroundings, setting down the cooler and collecting broken branches and sticks to make a fire.

Evie throws her voice.

> EVIE: *Ryan, where you at?*
> JOVAN: *Hey, I'm here.*
> EVIE: *These ice bags are freezing my fingers off.*
> JOVAN: *Follow my voice. Over here.*

One by one the trees roll out from behind themselves to become his friends.

> EVIE: *Oh, this is rad.*
> IAN: *This is hella dope!*

They all get super stoked. They drop the ice bags, charcoal and snacks, then help collect sticks to make a fire.

Once they get the fire going they celebrate, bro-ing out. Player D, Lana, runs back to the truck to get blankets and marshmallows. As she runs off, she immediately becomes the tree again. After a few seconds, the tree throws its voice.

> LANA: *Help!! Guys!! Help …*
> JOVAN: *Yeah, right, my dude!*
> IAN: *My dude's trying to scare us.*
> LANA: *No, I'm not kidding! Help!!*

Then the audience hears bloodcurdling screams.
> EVIE: *My dude's gotta stop!*
> JOVAN: *Yeah, he thinks he's going to scare us. We ain't scared.*

The silence is chilling.

IAN: *Trent?!*
EVIE: *Trent?!*

The remaining three get more and more concerned, huddling together near the fire.

JOVAN: *Trent?! My dude, stop playing!!*

A gust of wind blows out their fire. They freak out. Evie uses her lighter to try to see in the woods as she marches off past the single tree. It is very tense and very scary. All of a sudden, Evie runs back and then acts like she is being ripped back into the woods. She struggles, kicking and screaming as she's dragged away, and the others begin yelling, scared to death. Now there are two trees and two bros. This continues until all four players have vanished in the woods, returning to the initial tableau. Hold on it again. The boys in the distance can be heard wheezing, guttering, begging. They all scream facing their grisly death. A contagious of four monstrous growls echoes out of the woods followed by a dreadful silence. Lana throws her voice.

LANA: *One week later …*

The audience hears the crack of branches and the rustle of leaves. Ian spins around miming that they've just come from behind the tree, holding a flashlight.

IAN: *Found a campfire!*

One by one they're joined, rolling out from behind themselves to become the rest of the search party. A sheriff stares at the burned-out fire and the trees.

JOVAN: *Where in the hell did they go?*
EVIE: *What in the hell happened out here?*

Each sheriff and deputy is more baffled by the mystery than the next.

TIME DASH

Begin with two players creating a source scene based on a suggestion. Invite the performers to play patiently, set behaviors and strengthen their relationship until a game emerges organically. When it does, urge the players to heighten and pattern the fun of the scene.

Next, the players will *Time Dash* into a scene set in the past. This is an opportunity to pattern their characters' behaviors and relationships at an earlier time in a new location.

Remind players that this is a second beat, not a prequel. Although this explores the past, it does not mean players need to show how their characters first met. Like chess, playing is more fun than setting the board. Help players steer clear of this boring plot trap by doubling down on characterization and relationship. Set these scenes in a place in their past where their dynamic is the same, and they don't need formal introductions.

A bickering couple in the present scene may begin their time dash in the past by exchanging vows on their wedding day. It's not the moment they first met, but it does leverage their marriage and allows the audience to witness their charming and bickering vows.

Insist that players listen to their own scenes and specifics. If a touchstone moment is referenced in their source scene, such as — ***I should never have married you. I should have stomped off the altar and lit the limo on fire.*** — use it to explore and unpack their past.

Ultimately, this exercise sharpens characters' behavioral consistency through time.

Think of a super-cut of your favorite sitcom character; Stevie Janowski will always be Stevie, Elaine will be Elaine, Cartman is Cartman, Judy Gemstone is Judy Gemstone. The locations, scenarios and circumstances change from episode to episode, but the way they are, the way they move, stays consistent. This is their behavioral integrity. The Knight, the Bishop, the Pawns, the Queen — the configuration of the pieces on the board may change, but the rules to how these chess pieces move stay the same. Audiences enjoy picking up on these rules and behaviors and like seeing these character traits reinforced through time.

Simplicity is everything. There's no need to reinvent the wheel in the past, simply spin it one more time to see its function. Source scenes must be straightforward and clear. If characters are all over the place, nonsensical, bailing on their choices, it will be impossible for them to call anything back because there isn't a clear sense of who and how they were.

Players need to fail. Let them fail. Let source scenes spiral out of control so players learn to covet clarity in their characters. When the source scene is an absolute mess, invite the players to salvage what they can by picking a quirk, one fun thing, and sticking with it in their second beat. Simplicity acts as a defibrillator, reviving the scene by reinvesting in a character specific.

If after the second scene with all the notes and encouragement, there's still an identity crisis, let the scene fail and use it as a teaching opportunity to underline the tenets of improvisation.

Next, the players will *Time Dash* into the future. With success, the relationship is understood, and the behaviors are sharp and refined. There is zero hesitation or calculation: all flavor, no fat.

This exercise is excellent for developing the skills necessary for second beats, and tag-in formats such as the Evente and the Harold. It stresses the importance of establishing clear definitive character choices in the first beat so that there is a fun thing for players to return to and continue to invest in for subsequent beats.

This exercise can be tweaked to create second beats that revolve around character games as opposed to relationship or premise. Instead of showing the relationship of two characters through time, a single character would be plucked from the source scene and taken to a moment in their past by a different teammate, then taken to the future by another. This wedges open the exercise for the entire ensemble to explore a character's life and the different relationships that formed how they are and who they will become.

FLY IN THE ROOM – MONOSCENE

Begin by describing a sine wave. It starts ascending with positivity, then crests and slopes down, plummeting to a rock bottom before rebounding to repeat the wave again. The positive side is the A-side, and the negative side is the B-side.

Next, plot moments along this wave for players to follow. Start conversationally, establish normalcy, narrow in on something fun, heighten and react in kind until the scene crests, then a fly will buzz in, changing the temperature of the room. The players will drop their conversation to obsess and hunt the fly; they will swat it dead, then celebrate, returning to their conversation renewed and emboldened. This sequence of shared moments helps the players visualize the wave as a rollercoaster they can navigate and ride together.

Next, set six chairs on stage in a crescent and have players take a seat. Start establishing the A-Side with a group scene sharing true stories and opinions. The conversation should sprawl and ess, unpacking without efficiency. Players should be natural, inquisitive and real. They'll pull from their reality to build a base reality. Encourage them to listen to each other, make details matter, marinate on topics and fortify ideas that come up until they feel the conversation narrowing in on something. When it does, invite them to zero in on that topic. If something strikes funny, don't overthink it. Just have players repeat it and then share something similar. People do this naturally in life. At dinner, if someone has a band-aid, undoubtedly someone will ask what happened, and soon everyone is sharing their scar stories.

> JASON: *Oh my God!*
> SEAN: *You poor thing.*
> HARPER: *That's awful.*

Now players know what they're talking about (injuries) and how they feel about them (they're awful). Another player can reinforce this dynamic by sharing a similar story to elicit a similar reaction.

> JASON: *I severed my big toe. I was wearing flip-flops and dropped a propane tank right on it. It splatted like a cherry tomato.*

JORDAN: *Oh dear Lord in heaven.*
SEAN: *You poor thing.*
HARPER: *That's awful!!*

This is the A-Side, light, fun, riffing on broken bones and bad accidents. Pattern that lightness. Be more entertained by each person's story. These stories can build from a place of truth like the time you actually slammed your thumb in a car door, or be totally made up like the time you lost a leg from a motorboat propeller on Canandaigua Lake. Whatever the case, players must react and unpack each statement with more care, weight and importance.

As this pattern heightens, the A-Side will crest. At this moment, the instructor buzzes into the room, tracing the fly's path with their finger. A fly is used because it elicits an immediate and primal recoil. The ensemble feels the shift. The fly sours the fun, ripping players from their conversational high, plummeting to an invaded low.

Flipping from A-Side to B-Side, the players identify the fly, call it out, obsess over it, hunt it, and eventually kill it. When they slap it dead, they cheer. This celebration lifts them from hellbent extermination back to their joyful A-Side conversation, renewed and emboldened.

Advise each revisit to be played with more amplitude, higher highs and lower lows.

Challenge players to weave language from the A-side into their B-side and vice versa. After slapping the fly dead, someone may taunt the fly.

JORDAN: *Oh, too bad, no one will ever hear your scar story.*

Repurposing phrases and objects in this way helps the scene cohere. If players are nibbling on charcuterie in the A-Side, mount a fly's head on a toothpick as a pike to send a warning to all other flies to stay clear of the food.

As players ride this wave with more fluidity, prompt them to make new choices. Every entrance is a catalyst for the scene. Whether it's a pesky fly, a pitiful man in a leg cast, or a six-month-old corgi, walk-ons give characters an opportunity to reveal new sides of themselves. Urge players to co-sign and rally around the first reaction. Shared sentiment galvanizes the ensemble with immediacy and agreement. However, warn that blue doesn't show up on blue. If characters are angry and sniping on their A-Side, they can't be angry and sniping on their B-Side. It's too much of the same energy. It becomes grating.

Also watch for players who rush to kill the fly immediately, to get back to the fun of the A-Side. Note this right away. The entrance is there to rest the game. Records have two sides, *Wouldn't It Be Nice* and *God Only Knows*. The same Beach Boys, the same ensemble, but different songs. An audience needs a break to groove on something else so they can come back to the other song refreshed and excited to hear it again. The same is true of scenes. Rest the game with a new attitude, energy and spirit that pops in contrast to the A-Side.

Monoscenes can buckle under the weight of everyone entering with their own unique points of view, angling for attention and piling on information with very little connectivity.

A professional juggler doesn't kick off a show juggling twenty balls at once. There would be no room to grow. Instead, they take the stage with a single ball. They bounce it and catch it, then over their shoulder and catch it, then off the wall and catch it, then in the air and off the ground and off a wall and catch it. They keep building complexity until it's time to introduce a second ball. Monoscenes are a marathon, not a sprint. Use simplicity to be sophisticated. Begin these scenes with a single point of view: bounce those characters with one point of view off every surface there is, then when it's time introduce a second one.

> **Note:** For every unique point of view in a scene, players must allow at least two minutes of stage time for it to be established.

This Monoscene uses the Fly in the Room mechanics to streamline points of view, galvanize the players and establish a base reality. Every walk-on and exit allows characters, cut from the same cloth, to express new attitudes and opinions.

Set six chairs on stage in a crescent and have players take a seat. A seventh player will load offstage to enter later as *the fly*.

Assign a clear event for the players to attend, such as a Baby Shower. The players will set their A-Side with normal baby shower behavior, unwrapping gifts while being sweet to the expectant parent. Gifts can be unpacked for story and detail which helps the group identify who and how they are as characters. This creates a pattern for others to track with their gifts. Each present is met with more sweetness. When the A-Side dynamic crests, it's time to rest that energy with a walk-on.

The seventh player should feel the swell and need for something new. This entrance flips the energy to the B-side. They'll enter as a character with narrative significance and an energy of their own. They can dictate who and how they are, but the baby shower attendees will define how they feel about their character. Push the attendees to make a snap reaction the moment they enter. Let them lift or sour the room immediately with their presence. Often players do the opposite — they will wait to hear out a character's first line and then decide how they feel. Note this; it's more dynamic to see this choice made on a dime. Even when it doesn't make sense, a sharp choice made with confidence is arresting.

If it's a Grubhub driver delivering food, drown them in compliments, overtip them, invite them in and feed them your lunch.

When the B-side dynamic crests, it's time to rest that energy with the Grubhub driver leaving. Don't overstay your welcome. If you exhaust the game, it will exhaust the audience. Leave them wanting more.

When the delivery driver leaves, flip back to the A-Side with even more fun. Hit the game hard, and sing its chorus so that it is instantly recognizable to the audience. When possible, fold objects and language from one game into the other. With every revisit challenge the players to make discoveries.

> **Note:** If players try to individualize themselves too early, it will hijack the scene and can rattle the connectivity of the ensemble, fracturing all focus and restraint.

Example:

A character gives the expectant parent their brass baby rattle and explains that they can't have kids of their own so they wanted someone to have it. This is a sad, somber note that doesn't quite fit with the sweet enthusiasm that's been established with the A-Side dynamic. Revelations like this happen. Players can either swaddle the new information with sweetness and maintain the tone or use this detail to pivot to a new point of view, a C-Side, where the baby shower attendees all pity and console their friend and each other.

This sets three clear points of view for the ensemble to juggle and revisit: Sweetness, Flattery, and Consoling. After fifteen minutes, remove the governor and allow the ensemble to play the piece and follow the fun.

Drill these by offering events for dynamic scene starts: a college poetry class that has waited more than ten minutes for their teacher; a party bus on their way to Vegas; backstage before the very last production of a community theater that will be shut down tomorrow. These scenarios give players reps at establishing base realities with shared sentiment and clear points of view.

An alternate approach begins with all seven players on stage to establish the A-Side. As the scene crests, a character exits and the remaining six then reveal a new attitude for their B-Side. Each exit and entrance pivots the piece to a new spirit and energy. Done with sharpness, this elevates the Monoscene to feel and play out like a theatrical farce.

Assign a scene to use all these approaches together, such as a Secret Meeting at the Council of Elrond. Three players begin as tiny wood sprites. It is the first time they have been recognized by the council and they are unbelievably proud and grateful to be there. An elvish warrior enters and they lose all decorum. They swoon and beg for the elf's autograph. They are utterly starstruck. When the elvish warrior exits they collect themselves and temper their excitement. A sparrow enters. They immediately hiss and attack the curious bird, whom they see as a threat to Rivendell. Gandalf enters presenting the sprites with their cloaks and robes. They immediately become very judge-y of Gandalf and the robes, demanding they be altered. When Gandalf leaves, the sprites return to their seats full of pride and gratitude and feeling guilty for how they spoke to Gandalf.

Now that players have a clear sense of who and how they are in all of these points of view, they can enjoy playing the piece to pay off any conflict or fun.

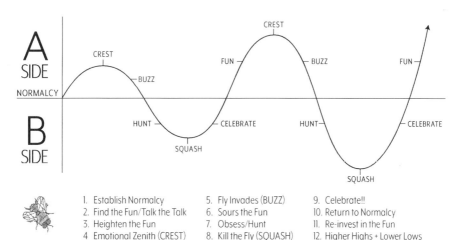

1. Establish Normalcy
2. Find the Fun/Talk the Talk
3. Heighten the Fun
4. Emotional Zenith (CREST)
5. Fly Invades (BUZZ)
6. Sours the Fun
7. Obsess/Hunt
8. Kill the Fly (SQUASH)
9. Celebrate!!
10. Return to Normalcy
11. Re-invest in the Fun
12. Higher Highs + Lower Lows

LONG
FORM
FORMATS

Long form formats give structure and shape to a piece. Some are rigid with rules and others amorphous and ethereal, but the games and relationships are found on the fly. Pieces can be vaudevillian, theatrical, Shakespearean and then on a dime shift gears, break the fourth wall, move from acoustic to electric to punk rock.

There are wonderful formats; The Monoscene, The Spokane, The Chicago Style Deconstruction, The Harold, Jazz Freddy, 4Track, Cat's Cradle, The Evente, The Throwaway, and JTS Brown, to name just a few. But these long form formats demand good bones.

Without strong scene work, all the structure, intricacies, beauty, special effects and cool transitions are for nothing. The formats fall flat and feel empty.

A format is just a form, the way a jar is just a jar. It's an empty vessel. It's what we put in the jar that defines it. It's a jar of strawberry jam, a jar of moonshine, or washers and bolts. Forms need the ensemble to fill it with their creativity, humanity, empathy, fears and years of experimentation and endorsing each other with trust and agreement, with poise and connectivity, to build worlds full of brilliant scenes and characters that make us laugh and think and feel.

Drill improv fundamentals with thoughtful lesson plans. The Warm-ups, drills, scene exercises, notes and metaphors should dovetail and fortify the aim of the rehearsal. There should be an identifiable arc throughout the lesson that culminates with a long form set. This allows students to use the muscle that was being isolated, on the fly, in real time, while playing a piece.

Each format requires different skills and strengths of the ensemble. Instructors must be able to deconstruct a format down to its simplest parts and help the ensemble under-stand how these integral components puzzle together to create hilarious pieces full of humanity.

MONOSCENE

The Monoscene takes place in one setting using theatricality and realism to bring torque, traction and stakes to the scene. The location inspires discoveries, characterization and relationships. The piece unfurls like a one-act play full of emotional shifts and narrative surprises.

We begin the Monoscene with two players talking about how goddamn cold it is. They roll out a plastic tarp and one starts stapling it to the floor. By the way they carry themselves, they seem blue-collar and rough around the edges.

> CHELSEA: *These condos just sit here empty for years, appreciating. Wish I could live in a place this nice.*
> NEIL: *I wouldn't want to live in a place that has this kind of history. Do you know how much paint must be on these walls?*

They are laying the groundwork for our scene, establishing who they are, how they are, what they are doing and why. We know they are goons, low on the totem pole. We know it's cold from the way they stand and keep breathing into their hands. We know this condo is better than anywhere they live. But based on how they're whispering, it seems maybe they shouldn't be there.

There's a slam from offstage and in a mad rush, Susan drags Ted in from the cold, yelling.

> SUSAN: *Shut the hell up! I'mma take your gag out your mouth so you can get some water. Just a little. Some drops. Get that tongue all slippery then you're going to let all them names slide out of your mouth, all of them.*

They set Ted on a chair in the center of the room. Susan yells at the other two:

> SUSAN: *What kind of plastic you buy? This isn't the thick stuff. If somebody's wearing boots they're going to rip the hell out of it! Then what?! All these cream-colored carpets gonna get stained with this dead man's blood. This poor tongueless thirsty bastard! His blood all over, you're gonna need a wet vac, a good one, and a goddam ocean's worth of club soda. Somebody get him some water!!*
> CHELSEA: *We don't have any water, the pipes aren't turned on.*
> NEIL: *The heat isn't even on.*

SUSAN: *Oh boo-fricking-hoo, cry me a river. This isn't a Jack Tar resort. This is a fricking kill house. Now get this dead man some water so he can start talking.*
CHELSEA: *There's some Canada Dry in the fridge.*
SUSAN: *Good, bring it over.*
NEIL: *But the fridge ain't plugged in so it's warm.*
SUSAN: *Then here, you do this.*

Susan marches to the door, opens it, grabs a handful of snow, squeezes it into a ball of ice shoves it down Ted's throat and puts the gag back on him.

SUSAN: *I'm gonna take this gag off, all right? Look at me.*

Susan slaps Ted across the face.

SUSAN: *Alright?! Answer me. You don't want to answer me. Okay!*

Susan pours soda into his mouth through the gag. Ted kicks and screams, gagging, gasping for air. As he struggles and kicks, the chair legs puncture the plastic tarp.

SUSAN: *See, look! What did I tell you? Gotta get another layer of plastic. Idiots.*

The scene escalates as these goons interrogate this guy on Christmas Eve.

Ted begs to go home and have one last Christmas with his family.

SUSAN: *You don't think we want to have Christmas? Don't you think we want to be home right now? Drinking egg nog out of a mug with antlers for the handles, with little ice cubes shaped like Christmas trees, huh? Huh?*

A gun is cocked and aimed at Ted's forehead, then ... ding dong.

Outside three carolers sing Christmas songs. The men hide the gun and open the door. They stand there listening, moved, touched. They each take stock of the year, their choices, and what they could've done to be somewhere else, somewhere warmer, somewhere with family. The moment the carolers leave, the door closes and they whip back to the same tense moment — the gun pushed harder against Ted's forehead. The goons wince in anticipation of the bullet.

> **Monoscene Components:** This Monoscene builds one brick at a time. Each gift chain links to a previous offer to build context and dimension, *Keep The ...* Every entrance shifts the status and temperature in the room, *Hitchhiker*. Characters match energies and opinions, paraphrasing and sharing sentiment, *Zhuzhing*. Everything they touch provides information, *Objects & Opinions*. They paint with the same brush. Beyond the mob and the guns, a sense of dread duty and regret builds to create a sinister underbelly. Then we get this pop of another color that cuts the darkness, resting the A-Side *Fly in the Room*. The carolers bring contrast and a reprieve from the dark. A shining Christmas light sings out, pure and joyful before it is snuffed out and the darkness returns more sinister, more taut, more empty.

CAT'S CRADLE

The Cat's Cradle is abstract and ever-changing, stirring themes, games, stories and characters into a thick soup of truth and humor. This form demands group ownership, bold choices, physicality, and split-second agreement.

When everyone is on the same wavelength, improv can be magical, especially working with an amorphous form like the Cat's Cradle which demands constant awareness of players, their moves, and their position.

Players must be open to hear the offers, inspiration, and where the piece leads them.

Think of the opening as seeding a garden. Players plant their scenes in certain areas: carrots downstage left, zucchini upstage right, summer squash upstage center, etc. Later in the piece, players may be downstage center playing a *Tomato Game*, then a character backs away into the zucchini plot allowing for the ensemble to pivot instantly to that new game. These little rabbit holes act as portals to warp into these new realities seamlessly.

Similarly, each character in the opening has an emotional tone: Proud Carrots, Frustrated Zucchini, Surprised Summer Squash, Sad Turnips, etc. If a supporting player is rejected in the *Carrot Scene* they may begin crying. Their sadness cuts through the proud room at a different frequency, permitting the ensemble to pivot to the *Sad Turnip Scene*.

Beyond using the real estate of the stage or emotional frequencies from within, players can also conjure these portals with language. Words have power. They summon and paint and invoke realities and callbacks and thread motifs.

The subconscious is so much more intelligent and creative than our conscious self.

Players often only pay attention to their conscious mind, and they miss all the subtle synergies and shared language that tie scenes, themes and worlds together. We must listen to our subconscious, give over to it, and let it guide us into a state of flow, where we are truly surprised and reach a transcendental connection.

If a scene starts with someone chaining themselves to a tree to stop a forest from being bulldozed, our subconscious mind will use words from that world later in the piece: Green, Timber, Oak, Pine, Sap, Leave, Chain, Root, Save, Nature, etc. When we hear ourselves using these words, it's as though the stage starts to shimmer and we can feel a thin space forming.

Thin space is a portal between the real world and the sacred world. For improv, it's where the walls of two scenes or universes butt up against each other. They are so close you can almost hear the other scene beckoning. It's like an eclipse where worlds align, allowing us to dive through the portal to get from one scene into another. Words unlock the connection in the audience's mind and help them see the outline of a window as it starts to shimmer. If a player dives through, inelegantly, the audience may not follow. Have patience; let the thin space form as a shimmering window. As words are repeated, the window grows to reveal a full doorway. Then charge through with intention before the door closes.

Think of a sorceress using her incantation to open the gates of a lonely mountain full of glittering caves. As she speaks, some of the glyphs begin to illuminate, then more, and then the entire doorway glows and opens. The idea here is that we knock on the door three times before entering the next scene, so as not to rush out of a scene prematurely. Instead, we earn the out. The previous scene builds to a crescendoed end and its power propels us to charge into the new scene.

This takes absolute focus and team awareness. Not only are they trying to do good scene work, but they are trying to thread a needle that opens and closes in a blink.

In a piece, a teacher begs their student to leave their room because it's Thanksgiving break, school ended an hour ago, and the teacher needs to catch a flight. However, the student doesn't understand why they missed one of the math problems. They insist on working through it to get it right. The rest of the ensemble supports the scene by being various objects in the teacher's room: an American flag in the corner, an overhead projector, a garbage can, etc. The teacher gets more and more frustrated. They begin straightening their room, putting up all the seats and throwing out a soda can a student left behind. It clunks in the garbage can. The student asks the teacher why the answer was wrong. The teacher balls the test up and throws it in the garbage can.

> TEACHER: *Don't worry about it! I'm going to give you full credit. Just, you've got to go!*

The student tries to pull the test from the garbage. The teacher raises their voice, totally fed up.

> TEACHER: *If you don't leave now, I'm going to miss my flight, and there goes my whole weekend. Gone! Right in the trash! Is that what you want? Huh, want me to throw everything out?! Huh?!*

The teacher begins throwing books and papers into the trash, yelling at the top of their lungs. Then they throw the kid's backpack into the trash can. At this moment, the scene is white hot. All the physical and emotional energy is being aimed at the trash can, creating a thin space. The player, playing the garbage can, begins humming classical music, charging the school scene with drama. Then the flag and overhead projector begin humming as well, and the student and teacher begin humming. The garbage can rises with its arms still in a hoop and they begin dancing a ballet. The rest of the ensemble quickly moves to support, pulling the players, the objects, and the audience through the thin space and into an entirely new scene at the ballet.

> **Cat's Cradle Components:** *Spotlight Hydraulic, Dagger & Hair, Build a Band, Character Context, Ranting & Raving, Two-Headed Monster, The Audition, Cul de Sac, Vines, Ordinary Extraordinary, Pivot Edits, Toy Chest.*

4TRACK

The 4Track form demands that players rush the stage with confidence and connectivity. It revels in ensemble and is played with abandon. Matching scenes ratchet the energy building to a boil before tumbling into an avalanche of sharp callbacks. This form rejoices in bold choices, physicality, and split-second agreement.

Four players take a suggestion and rush the stage with a matching scene in which they are all cut from the same cloth. They assimilate each other's choices, champion each other, share every gift and finish each other's sentences. The level of agreement and speed should be arresting. These matching scenes may start grounded but they are designed to exaggerate and pull from truth to create characters and then stretch them to a point of caricature and commentary. The scene should feel like a wave of energy that comes crashing at the audience, and when it recedes, two players are left on the stage like seashells.

The two players hold on to some extraction from the previous matching scene — a physicality, a quote, a mantra, or a theme — and use it to inspire a patient, two-person, un-matching scene, full of heat and weight. These scenes are behavioral, less game-y and more lived-in. The characters and humor come from their realness and their wants. If the matching scenes are cartoonish, these are anchored. The contrast is glaring, giving the piece brightness and consequence. Think, *Who Framed Roger Rabbit*, *Merrie Melodies* meets *Chinatown*.

That two-person scene may lead to a tag run following the fun, or develop into a monoscene with walk-ons before it is edited boldly with another four-person matching scene that is inspired by a brand-new take on the suggestion. And that scene hits like another wave, and when it recedes, two new players are left on stage to begin another patient, two-person un-matching scene.

These tidal shifts occur four times, giving us four disparate currents running through our show, and between them rest three grounded scenes with weight and stakes. In the fourth and final matching scene, we let the energy swell and lift the scene into a frenzy, then organically transform into other moments from the show, creating an avalanche of callbacks, each revisitation sharper, the relationships more pronounced, the games more distilled. It is important not to overstay the welcome on the way up the mountain. Just as the arrow is released from the bow and the arrow screams through the air —edit. Then in the final moments of the piece arrow after arrow can hit the

target, one last cymbal crash of their character games, tying up any loose narrative threads to create a crescendoed finale.

> **4Track Components:** *Spotlight Hydraulic, Cooey Cooey Cooey, Character Context, Ranting & Raving, Take Off Scenes, Pea in a Pod, Slow Burn, The Audition, Cul de Sac, Vines, Flocking, Pivot Edits, Toy Chest, Character Waltz.*

LIGHTS OUT

Essentially, this is a dynamic freeze tag. Every scene is edited with a blackout. When the lights are out the performers shuffle in or out, then strike a new pose on stage. When the lights come up, the performers quickly wrangle the scene by justifying their positions, triangulating a context based on proximity, stage picture and eye contact.

It's a dance of daggers and ribbons.

Whoever is in the booth running lights is not only editing but setting the tempo of the piece. Variation in scene length is crucial. No one likes a Fourth of July where every firework is exactly the same color, sound and placement in the sky. The audience wants variety and wonder. The booth must intuit when to give certain scenes room to grow and when others can be blacked out after a pithy two-line scene.

This montage has zero room for pre-planning. Everything is discovered the moment the lights come up. Players must embrace the unknown, read each other's faces and make sense of what presents itself. Those who fight to shoehorn their ideas into the piece stick out like a sore thumb. The more they cling to their ideas for control the more phony and contrived it feels.

These pieces help remedy heady over-thinkers who script their scenes instead of being in the moment. Awaken their ability to seamlessly drop whatever they saw for whatever was said first and run with it.

These scenes begin bizarre and weird. That's all the chaos a piece needs. Now players have to build a context for it, a way it makes sense, a rationale that rings true and grounds it.

Castles in the sky need a staircase to ground them.

It's the player's job to find order and patterns and meaning in this confusion and when they do to heighten the hell out of it.

Players must commit to their scenes. They can't sell out, hoping for a blow line because that blackout might not come. They must invest in the reality and keep grinding whether the edit is there or not.

Good editing is everything. It's punctuation. But if a team doesn't earn the edit, then they're just using it to bail themselves out of their scene, to surrender. It's a white flag instead of an exclamation point. When you feel boxed in and don't know how to grow the scene, you edit. When you don't know what to say, edit. You get a single laugh that might've actually been a sneeze, edit. Players love hearing the audience clap, but everyone knows the difference between a pity clap and actual applause. Use your edits correctly, and don't bail on your scenes.

This format puts the edit in the hands of the instructor and allows them to really push the ensemble to grow and invest in their scenes until there is an out. Players can't shrug and wait for an edit. This keeps them moving, pushing forward, growing momentum and thinking about ways to sustain a scene, even when they think it should be edited. This is an incredible dessert piece, especially following a form that's anchored in premise-heavy play. Every scene reminds the audience that this is 100% improvised. The audience shares the player's blindfold and witnesses the brilliance of the ensemble making sense of it all. They delight when players glom onto the same idea and justify through the same lens to bring order and dimension to the plum pudding mess. It is an exhilarating, death-defying crowd-pleaser.

A drawback to this type of piece is that people can hide, deferring to other players to take care of the scene for them. Note that. First, share the observation with the ensemble, then invite them all to be more proactive and responsible for the piece. If the hiding continues, adjust by running a fifteen-minute set where the instructor calls a player's name in the darkness indicating it's their job to wrangle the next scene when the lights come up. This ensures all players develop this muscle and not just the fastest or boldest of the bunch.

> **Lights Out Components:** *Land, Look & Speak, Road Trip, Emotional Landmines, Action & Reaction, Pass the Phrase.*

ORGANIC MONTAGE

This can be played with or without an opening. Openings act as a preamble, introducing themes, motifs, behaviors and games inspired by a suggestion. Players pull ideas from this subconscious stew, so they can start scenes with actionable games ready to play. In this example, five players will field a suggestion and use it to create a Daisy Chain, a short opening, where players *A to C* off the suggestion and off each other to create a chain of free-associative words like a garland of daisy flowers threaded together by the stems.

This barebones opening is a prism. The ensemble shines a white light that is the audience's suggestion through the opening, and it fractures into distinct colors. It is the players' job as an ensemble to witness every color so they can paint with those colors in their scenes.

The suggestion is vanilla. Everyone repeats vanilla.

Pete goes A to C off Vanilla.
In their head synapses fire in a few milliseconds. They are thinking: A is vanilla. Vanilla makes me think of cookies. B is Cookies. Cookies make me think of Baker's Dozen. C is Baker's Dozen.
Pete then says, Baker's Dozen.

Jen now goes A to C off Baker's Dozen.
In their head synapses fire: Baker's Dozen > Munchies > Bong Rip
Jen says Bong Rip.

Amber goes A to C off Bong Rip.
Bong Rip > R.I.P. > Tombstone
Amber says, Tombstone.

Emma goes off Tombstone.
Tombstone > Shotgun > Pregnant Bride
Emma says, Pregnant Bride.

Dean goes off Pregnant Bride.
Pregnant Bride > Kill Bill > Tarantino
Dean says, Tarantino.

Once each player has said their word or phrase, the rest of the ensemble looks at each player as everyone repeats theirs.

Vanilla - Baker's Dozen - Bong Rip - Tombstone - Pregnant Bride - Tarantino - Vanilla

This repetition reinforces each concept and tethers it to its initiator. A player's recall is much better when players actually look and listen to each other.
Next, they begin their montage to unpack their concepts and celebrate each other. Pete will explore Baker's Dozen, and Jen will explore Bong Rip, and so on.

Pete runs to a stationary player, and grabs at their elbow, flinging them open like a refrigerator door. Pete fills his arms with eggs, milk, and butter bringing them downstage and setting them on a counter as they giggle. He runs to another player who becomes a pantry door. He fills his arms again with flour, sugar and baking soda, even more giddy. He measures flour into a bowl, then sugar then vanilla then licks his finger with delight. Pete runs to another player picking strawberries and rhubarb and ginger. They cut the fruit into a pie and then cross downstage to place it in the oven. Heavenly smells fill the kitchen. Pete swallows, hungry. He licks his lips and stares at the pie as it bakes, shaking his head trying to have patience. The caramelized sugar beckons. The supporting players beckon with their fingers. Pete is drawn to the smell but fights it until he can't anymore. Pete yanks open the oven and begins eating the pie with his fingers, burning and licking, showing his pain and ecstasy. The stage picture is combustible — this is the literal sweet spot, use its power to erupt to a new idea. Pete continues to heighten and throws powdered sugar around the room and runs trying to catch it on his tongue like snow. He dives to the floor and begin making powdered sugar snow angels.

Amber charges forward, as a doctor to honor Tombstone, looking at Pete and checking her watch.

> AMBER: *Time of death ... 2:19 pm.*

The room goes somber.

Pete shuts his eyes making a flat-line noise. In an instant, the rest fill out a hospital room. The Doctor, Amber, stares at the dead man, wishing she could've done more.

> AMBER: *Nothing I do is ever right!*

To swaddle Amber with context, Dean enters, yelling.

> DEAN: *Doctor! Doctor! We need help!*

Amber runs to the next room where a man is choking.

> DEAN: *I just gave him a peppermint and I think it went down the wrong pipe.*

Amber tries the Heimlich but breaks the choking man's ribs.

JEN: *My rib!*

Amber helps the man into a chair who immediately falls off the chair, making the flat-line noise.

AMBER: *C'mon!*

Amber feels cursed with the hands of a Grim Reaper. Even with the best intentions they cannot help but bring death everywhere they go.

EMMA: *Oh, hey, Doctor Cohen, did you want to get in on this Super Bowl pool?*

As soon as Amber looks at her colleague, they flatline.

JEN: *Psst, we got Denise a cookie cake; we're all about to sing Happy Birthday.*

Amber joins in singing. As Pete blows out her candles, everyone drops dead like a house of cards, making a flat-line noise. Amber fills with existential strife and balls up in the fetal position, shaking, miserable, desperate and scared.

In this emotionally charged moment, Emma sees a window to alley-oop Jen's idea. Emma crosses to the crouching doctor and transforms her into a bong.

EMMA: *All right, everyone check this out, this is the biggest bong I've ever packed.*

They point to Jen.

EMMA: *Here, who wants first?*

Jen immediately registers this as their idea. She shakes her head.

JEN: *I don't know, I've never smoked before. Are you sure it's okay? It seems like a lot. Like a lot of weed.*

Jen takes a rip off the bong and the ensemble works together to make it the most magical experience of the person's life. All their worry and concern melt away. They have a transcendental awakening full of bliss, angelic voices sing to them, and then all at once, it's over.

Jen scrambles to smoke more and more, shrooms, ecstasy, angel dust. They are chasing the dragon, trying to get back to the best high of their life. This elevates to commentary about addiction and escapism, pleasure and pain. Jen overdoses and one of her hippie friends, Emma, yells for help.

EMMA: *She's wigging out! Is there a doctor in the house?*

And of course, the only doctor in the piece has the touch of death.

This is just three scenes of an organic montage to get the feel of its energy, fluidity and mechanics. It's essential in this work to grab the energy and immediately package ideas and movement in a way that confidently communicates to the rest of the ensemble that you are shifting from the previous scene to the next. Wishy-washiness creates static and confusion for everyone, including the audience.

Speak with authority.

Grab the energy with importance. Move with your idea and include your ensemble so they can swaddle and support you in an informed and meaningful way.

Note: As the form evolves, players must recalibrate their sensitivity. They don't want to be so sensitive that any time someone breathes it cues the ensemble to abandon their present scene. The team needs to feel that crescendo and let it launch into the next idea. This demands clarity and discipline from each player to pick up on every subtlety and intention.

Organic Montage Components: *Vines, Toy Chest, Snow White Scenes, Character Waltz, Pivot Edits.*

IMPRO-VISERS & INSTRUC-TORS

WORKING WITH A TEAM AS A COACH

Before committing to coach a team long term, meet with them to see where they're at, how they work together, and if there's synergy between instructor and ensemble.

Have them meet outside of rehearsal and identify their goals as a team:

We want to be fun-chasing improvisers who hit the game hard.
We want to do grounded, patient scene work that gives way to absurdity.
We want to do trippy organic pieces with total confidence.

Next have each player answer the following questions and discuss with their team:

How big of a priority is this team?
Are you interested in being recreational, semi-professional or professional?
How many hours a week do you want to dedicate to this group?
Do you care about scene work, formats, individual growth?

Encourage honesty and not fearing to hurt anybody's feelings. If someone is busy and sees this as a low priority, they should say that. If someone is gung-ho and wants everyone to devote two nights a week to rehearsals and doing shows and touring, they should say that.

Having these talks upfront is healthy. It gets unsaid expectations out in the open. Those who are entirely out of alignment with the majority will see it, and that is okay. It may seem like people are only a few degrees out of alignment, but over time those slight difference can bring us a world away from one another, and then frustration and resentment creep in. Better to name it early than to let it rip apart the team and waste everyone's time, energy and money.

If there is zero alignment; if everyone has a wildly different agenda; if some are there to get reps; others want to do shows; and others have no interest in performing but want to do better pattern games in class, that is not a team. If they cannot agree to play with a shared objective and approach, then it will be impossible for an instructor to tailor each rehearsal to each person's own bespoke wants.

If they can't see the writing on the wall for themselves, the instructor needs to be direct. Be firm to be kind. Life is short. Don't spend your time surrounded by the wrong people. Make use of the time that you are investing and don't settle. Group with like-minded like-hearted people and march toward a shared goal.

At the start, take a few minutes with the ensemble to brainstorm and establish clear rules for rehearsals:

No phones
No food
Be on time ready to move and ready to be present
Be ready to try things and fail and succeed
Be intentional
Be open to notes
Be humble and hungry to learn
Be kind to yourself and to your teammates

This serves as another opportunity for a group to align expectations. When rules are created by committee, it keeps everyone accountable.

TEACHERS & COACHES

Teachers use a curriculum to platform a school's methods, core principles, foundational tenets and concepts for its students. Coaches are hired to help a team get additional reps, practice skills, and become the best ensemble possible.

If you want to coach improv but at this point you feel like you might not know enough to do it, you're probably right. Within the improv world there are very few standards. Anyone can get on stage and say they're a performer. Anyone who feels like coaching can coach. No one can question anyone's claims. Without standards, we are ruining the art form we love in order to pretend we're something more than we are.

Anyone who wants to start being paid to coach needs to have an expertise at it.

No one would hire a personal trainer who just joined the gym and started working out a week ago. But this happens in the improv world. People take a course that meets for three hours, once a week, for eight weeks, with sixteen people in the class where you get up roughly half the time. To be generous, that's 12 hours of improv instruction. Let's say that these people have more of a conscience and wait until they complete a six-level program before they decide to coach. That's 72 hours of improv. And let's say that those people are part of a practice group and they've done ten shows. That's 150 hours of improv. That is less than a week's worth of time. Anyone who claims to be an expert at anything after doing it for less than a week is delusional.

On stage, Improv is about embracing the unknown, but that does not apply to teaching the art form. Get the reps you need by being upfront and forthcoming with groups.

> ASPIRING COACH: *I don't have enough hours to be an expert at this, but I am passionate and want to learn. I will put in the time and work with your group for free over the next four weeks. The only thing I ask is that you give me feedback at the end of the four weeks and let me know honestly what resonated with you, what you liked, what I could do better, etc.*

This shows dedication to the craft and how direct and honest you can be with them. I did this for the first few months in New York City. One group turned into two, turned into four, and soon I had five hundred hours of coaching. That's not a lot, but I could feel my notes become more pointed, my lesson plans more sophisticated, and eventually teams insisted on paying me for my time and expertise.

Don't sell out the craft to make a couple bucks. Set standards for yourself and your community. Titles and words mean nothing without definition. Define what it is to be a dedicated coach by putting in the work and leading by example.

TYPES OF IMPROVISERS

There are certain Improv Types that can delay or derail a lesson. It is important to neutralize these behaviors early to keep focus, balance and momentum in the room.

SUPER FANS

In rehearsal, they geek out about improv, about your teammates, about moves they saw you make on stage, about getting tickets to your next show. This is flattering, and awkward. They quiz you to see if you remember certain shows from years back. And tell you that you are the reason they started doing improv. It's amazing, but it shouldn't be the reason they are in the room with you. They should be there to work and if you allow it to be about you, you've already derailed the agenda of the rehearsal. Wrangle this energy.

> INSTRUCTOR: *I'm flattered. These are all really kind words, but we're here to work. If you want to talk after class when you're not paying to do that... I'm all for it, but I would much rather use this time to put in the work so you can inspire other people in the future when they see you perform.*

This is hopefully all they need to re-calibrate and focus on rehearsal.

However, sometimes these fans can be intimidated and nervous about doing bad work in front of their *improv idols*. Flattery becomes a delay, their shielding tactic. If they don't work, they can't fail. If the flattery continues, double down on your stance. Always remember to do this with kindness.

> INSTRUCTOR: *Listen, I really want this to be a productive rehearsal, so as much as I appreciate the kind words, let's get to work.*

Then throw to a warm-up that's abstract or physical to get them out of their heads.

If this pattern persists and each week they're just eating into their own rehearsal time, the instructor needs to say something.

> INSTRUCTOR: *Hey, I appreciate that you appreciate my work. I've asked that we not let that distract us from why we are here. If I'm not making myself clear, then maybe I'm not the instructor for you. I hope that's not the case because I love working with you and want to help you be as great as you can be. If this continues moving forward, I'll have to step down as your coach.*

Ninety-nine out of hundred times they will hear this and take it to heart. It goes a long way toward showing your professionalism and how respectful you are of them and their time.

THE STEAMROLLER

A Steamroller barrels through scenes, barely listening, out for a laugh, never building, just bulldozing their own path, trampling gifts, leaving their teammates in their dust to pick up the pieces.

Some Steamrollers are hilariously gifted performers, most are not. Both need noting.

When the strongest player on a team is a Steamroller, cite their confidence as a strength. Highlight their natural instincts and genius and then explain that you want to help them to trust and celebrate their ensemble. Challenge the rest of the room to be just as dynamic and confident. Most players will be flattered, thankful and welcome the notes.

Instructors must drive home the need for connection. Plowing through a scene doesn't have the same impact as building a scene together. A Steamroller must learn to embrace their partners' offers and use their own imagination to make their scene partner's ideas take flight.

Invite the strong player to be the first to demonstrate new exercises and dial your notes to be more exacting. Having the fearless player lead gives timid, less confident performers a chance to see the exercise before they try. Invite others to improve upon the work and incorporate the notes. This repurposes the Steamroller into a trailblazer for the team. Otherwise, the player sits, judging their teammates' struggle, feeding the narrative that their teammates are *less than* and cannot be trusted. When a strong player hops up after twenty minutes of lackluster work and delivers a great scene, this only evidences the talent disparity, fracturing the team further.

An instructor uses the strengths of the individuals to inspire and strengthen the team. A savvy player working with performers who are too hesitant will breed impatience and lack of trust in the group. A strong player recognizes that the team can't handle their offers, and instead of slowing down, they barrel through. Instead of engaging in a give and go dialogue with their teammate, they throw the focus against the back board and alley-oop themself for a double clutch dunk.

This all comes down to fear. They don't trust their scene partners. When performers are scared, they cling to familiarity and control. They know they can get a laugh on their own, so they do it. The more success they have doing it, the harder it becomes to break the habit. Call it out. Tell them that you will be hard on them, because you want them to learn to play with others, not just be stuck in their own bulldozed rut fueled by fear and trust issues.

If a Steamroller doesn't change their ways, encourage them to meet one on one with each of the members of their team and do a half an hour in a room and then go get dinner. No audience. No selling out their scene partner for a laugh. Just reps to build familiarity and trust with each other. The more faith they have in the ensemble, the more patience they can have with the ensemble on stage.

Unfortunately, most Steamrollers are not the strongest. Their instincts are actually bad. The moves they make muddle what's going on and for some reason it doesn't phase them. They're more brazen. They may contest notes:

STEAMROLLER: *You just don't understand the future of comedy the way I do.*

This is a very particular type of player, the self-proclaimed Comedic Visionary. Take the time to help them; they need an instructor's patience as much as they need a reality check.

INSTRUCTOR: *You might see things that we don't, but comedy needs context. It needs to be recognizable to the audience in order for it to resonate. You can't just leap into the future. Give us the baby step to start us on that journey with you. Otherwise it will always seem confusing and a little off. Help your teammates and the audience understand what you're doing, what you're going for, by giving us a few steps in the right direction before you hit the turbo button.*

This approach is generous and gives them the benefit of the doubt. It invites them to align with others and bring clarity to their work.

The ensemble can now trust that the instructor has an eye on the Steamroller's tendencies and will appreciate them trying to corral it with tact. The goal is to identify if the rogue player is willing to change. If they genuinely take the notes to heart, amazing. Continue being firm and patient.

If they nod feigning agreement but are still stubborn and stuck in their ways, stick with it for the next three to four rehearsals. Be pointed and positive with your notes. Help them understand that their steamrolling and deflections are likely a defense mechanism. By being *ahead of their time* they never have to face their present failings. Communicating this lesson can be a Sisyphean task because any notes or adjustments are triggering for them. It sends them into fight or flight where they will do anything to preserve how they feel about their work, their choices, and themself. They do anything they can not to listen.

If after weeks of encouragement there's no change, or worse, resistance, address the player and their reluctance in front of the ensemble.

> INSTRUCTOR: *For the past few months, I've invited you to take the notes and encouraged you to align with your teammates, but there doesn't seem to be a desire to change or listen. Your unwillingness to try hijacks our rehearsals, the work and any opportunity to grow as an ensemble. We're at a standstill. As an instructor, I need everyone's ears and trust for my feedback to carry any weight. As an ensemble, each player needs to respect each other and push themselves to improve in order for us to continue to grow. I would not be doing my job if I did not address this. As a team, it's time to meet and decide if your priorities have changed or if it's time for a new instructor, or if we all want to continue to work and grow and hold each other accountable. I care about you, your time and the art too much to let us just keep drifting along.*

THE ACOLYTE

For an Acolyte watching a great improv show for the first time, witnessing the trust and synergy of an ensemble lift the room is a revelation. It's a religious experience. It draws people in. They enroll, and dedicate themself to that school of thought. They become loyal fans, worshiping the stage and the performers. They hold the school's philosophies with a devout intensity. The teacher's lessons become gospel. The way scenes are devised becomes dogma. Anything that challenges this is blasphemous. Unchecked, this person can become an adoring zealot.

> ACOLYTE: *I really liked the way you noted us. It was exactly what we needed to hear. You're so on it. You see everything. We're in such good hands.*

It feels good when someone has faith in you as a teacher, when they actually write down what you say and nod along with your notes. It's validating, especially to new coaches who might feel insecure or suffer from imposter syndrome. Be careful. Over time, this type of student may get bolder.

This may be the only class where they've ever felt comfortable in scenes and on stage. When people go through life feeling ignored, unheard or misunderstood, it feels incredible when an instructor is there to watch, and listen in earnest, and lift them up. They can't fathom where this feeling is coming from, how they reached these heights. Obviously, it is from the trust and connection you are fostering in the classroom. But instead of giving themself and their teammates the credit, they project it onto you, their teacher. You made this possible.

The instructor becomes their shepherd, a saint, then a symbol. It's impossible to live up to the perfection they are painting. Call it out.

INSTRUCTOR: *I'm glad this approach speaks to you, but there are so many others out there that are equally as valid. As an improviser, don't fixate on one path. Embrace other techniques to become a well-rounded performer.*

Drive home that the excitement and confidence they feel stems from the trust they have in the ensemble and the skills they've developed as an individual. This neutralizes any mania that would come from them saying that your way is the only way. Be diligent. Make this clear to the individual and reiterate to the class. Nip it before they begin to project onto you, the instructor, what they believe; assigning quotes to you that you've never said; reading between the lines of your lessons, all while singing your praises.

Devotion can easily become delusion. A simple note given on an off day can devastate them; they spiral into self-flagellation mode, beating themselves up or worse, they feel betrayed by you and instead of taking the note they turn on you, and all the holes they filled with love and adoration turn into hate and resentment. They feel abandoned by you, scorned. And in a snap the zealot becomes a heretic.

Find ways to constantly reference other people, where you got your lessons from, how this is a shared improv language and craft and not your lessons alone. This helps this type of student to see that there is no one way to do the art form that we love.

THE ASSISTANT COACH

In almost every elementary school, there is a child who delights in helping the teacher, handing out papers, taking attendance, erasing the board, etc. In moderation this is a wonderful ally to have in a classroom or on a team. Imagine a teammate who takes copious notes and posts them to a shared document online for others to reference and review. This studious approach honors the work and the art with reverence.

However, when these instincts are less altruistic and more self-serving, it can create a destructive environment. This type of player finds self-importance by tethering to the teacher, parroting notes, or citing other teachers at every opportunity. Ensemble players must be equal in the classroom. They must all be malleable and open to learning and taking the notes in order to operate as a team. If a fellow performer clings to power by repeating or paraphrasing the lesson, noting their peers, or stopping scenes to give direction or clarify, they destroy the balance in the room. Address it immediately. Judgement breeds tension and self-conscious play. If members of a group feel they are being watched, critiqued or judged by their teammates, this will poison the well, making it difficult for anyone to let their guard down and play freely.

> INSTRUCTOR: *I appreciate your desire to clarify for others but when you interject, it complicates and confuses the ensemble's dynamic. Please trust that I will offer clarity when it is needed. My role as instructor is to keep a watchful eye on you as a group, so that none of you needs to carry any responsibility other than being playful and open with each other. You can drop your shields and any criticisms and just be present in order to learn and grow.*

Selfless players will take this for the invitation it is. Selfish players may prickle at it.

> ASSISTANT COACH: *But you weren't calling it! They keep making the same mistake! I could tell they weren't getting it and you weren't saying anything.*

Note this right away.

> INSTRUCTOR: *Trust that I see what needs noting and will note it when the time is right. If you do not have confidence in my abilities, then perhaps I am not the right coach for you.*

Being this blunt in a public manner will hopefully reset the balance of the room.

Unchecked, this type of player wastes time peacocking, debating improv semantics, keeping things theoretical instead of taking in the notes on a personal level. Worse, their encyclopedic knowledge of improvisation language makes them bulletproof to notes.

> INSTRUCTOR: *You weren't Yessing your scene partner's ideas. In fact, you were creating road blocks for your scene.*
> ASSISTANT COACH: *You're not suppose to judge our work. You said yourself judgement squelches the creativity in the room.*

They deflect and justify their mistakes by twisting improv quotes to shirk responsibility. They use *what they know* not to grow and experiment but to defend their bad choices.

They don't want to feel judged. So they turn improv rules and logic into legalese to make a case for themself and prove they were in the right. Help them use their creativity to create on stage, not to defend and dismiss notes meant to make them a better player and teammate.

DILLYDALLY-ERS

Rehearsals should be productive. Call out people who drag their feet and roadblock momentum. If the entire team is sluggish, if someone reclines in their seat or lies on the floor, if no one ever shows up on time, and others have to leave early — it must be addressed.

Entrances and exits suck all the energy out of the room because the instructor constantly has to re-explain everything. This creates a black hole. Rehearsals become a time suck.

> INSTRUCTOR: *All right, let's get everybody up on their feet!*
> TEAMMATE 1: *Oh, hold on, I want to change my shoes.*
> TEAMMATE 2: *Is it okay if I go to the bathroom real quick while they're doing that?*
> TEAMMATE 3: *Did we all pay? Because I think I forgot to pay last week.*

Everyone is operating on their own terms, so there is zero sense of ensemble. Note this with kindness and candor.

> INSTRUCTOR: *I love you guys, but when we have to start and stop class, when we don't take care of business before rehearsals, that eats into all of our time. You said you want to be committed and disciplined about this, but that's not*

happening. When one of us dillydallies, it shows that we don't have respect for everyone else's time. Maybe an adjustment can be made so it doesn't feel like our schedules are stacked against us. As your coach, I want more for you than this.

Similar to Super Fans, Dillydally-ers may be afraid of doing bad scenes so they delay getting to work or avoid coming to rehearsal altogether. They may be someone who loves watching improv but doesn't like doing it.

Just because you like going to an improv show doesn't mean you need to be an improviser. People may love going to the movies and eating popcorn, but that does not mean they should be a film maker. Don't confuse these things.

If the members of the team share a recreational passion for learning improv, it is the coach's job to calibrate rehearsals appropriately. Keep the stakes low and the rehearsals fun and simple.

If they insist they want to be professional, then be truthful.

INSTRUCTOR: *If you want to be professional, then we need to act like professionals and we need to change the rehearsal time, moving forward so everyone can arrive five minutes early, ready to work. That means settle dues on a dedicated day outside of our rehearsal time; only go to the bathroom in the event of an emergency; silence or turn off phones during rehearsal, so that when we're here we can be 100% focused on being the best ensemble possible.*

IMPROV NERDS

Maybe someday the art form grows to a point where comedy institutions offer Improv History as an elective, where the class discusses Commedia Dell' Arte, the Compass Players, Del Close and Keith Johnstone and Viola Spolin. They would map formats and trace why they emerged sociologically and unpack improv philosophies and psychology. As niche and fascinating as it would be, instructors can't allow a rehearsal to fall down these academic sink holes, waxing for hours about history without doing any actual work.

When you are on a basketball court you practice and play basketball, you don't spend the two hours you rented the court to discuss MJ, or who would be on your Mt. Rushmore of NBA greats. The same is true of rehearsals. Improv exists as live theatre; it must

Improv: The Art Of Collaboration

be rehearsed to be honed. Students are paying for your expertise on how to work as a team. Keep that aim in mind. When students ask questions that veer the rehearsals back to these symposium-like dialogues, call it out.

> INSTRUCTOR: *I could talk about this stuff forever, but we're here to work, so let's hop up!*

Another option is to grab coffee with the team after rehearsal when they are not paying for a room and continue the discussion then. Most of the time this doesn't happen, because this type of player gravitates to these conversations because it's sophisticated, it feels like learning, and they never have to take the risk of failing in front of their classmates. It is a way for them to be passionate, scholarly and serious about improv with zero chance for embarrassment.

If rehearsals continue to devolve into these eddying academic talks, be very clear.

> INSTRUCTOR: *I've mentioned this before. I love talking shop like this but I'm here to coach and work with you as an ensemble. As I see it, we have two options. We can change our aim and make this more of an improv discussion group and instead of renting a room we could meet at a restaurant, or we keep our aim and I will designate twenty minutes for discussion to every class, so that we can unpack the exercises we are drilling in this academic way.*

CONTROL FREAKS

Great improv is fearless. Performers must be vulnerable and open to uncovering the bold, ugly ridiculousness of humanity.

Instead of being brave and free associative, scared players demand control, that others play by their rules and their rules alone. Their experience supersedes everyone else's, even the audience's.

> CONTROL FREAK: *I don't want any surprises. I want to know exactly what's going to happen at all times. I don't want to support anything that I don't believe in politically, morally, or ethically. I will only play myself and things that I am comfortable playing. I don't want people playing anything other than themselves because I want to know that I can trust these people. And don't be dragons or aliens. I don't like that stuff. Oh and also, I don't want to have to be a tree or an animal. Don't tag me out mid-sentence cause that's just rude. Don't tell me what to do. I don't like fighting scenes unless I'm winning. And I definitely don't want to be shot in the face.*

This is not an improv mindset.

Imagine this same player wanting to be a clown, but they don't want to wear a red nose or big shoes, or get sprayed with water, and they definitely don't want people laughing at them. It would be pretty clear to everyone that this person isn't a clown. But improv exists in a world of pretend; other than two cafe chairs there's nothing tangible, so it's very easy for players to delude themselves and pretend they are an improviser.

Their laundry list of demands to control squelches any potential fun or discovery. If an instructor allows an individual to dictate the rules of the work, it erodes the ensemble and narrows the scope, restraining the others, confining creativity. This becomes a slippery slope. In fairness, if we cater to the rules of one, then we should cater to each person's preferences, which narrows the playing field even further. Now the impulse is gone from the play. Instead declarations are met with calculating eyes, computing the correct response instead of the inspired one.

Our infinite playground is reduced to a one foot by one foot sandbox. Controlling players want to shrink the world so that they can feel like a giant. They can feel in control. They can pretend they are an improviser. Note this right away — Players can limit themselves but they should not feel entitled to limit everyone else. This is an overstep. There is a difference between establishing and maintaining boundaries as addressed earlier, and trying to control everything and everyone.

Comedy is about discomfort. Without bite, or danger, when nothing has an edge, there is no commentary. Don't Nerf the work. On stage we will likely be embarrassed, and the show will have ups and downs, ebb and flow, glory and failure. Staying where it's safe for our characters and ourselves is boring to watch. An instructor must help these players and the ensemble understand that our playground ranges from the deepest parts of human experience to the furthest reaches of the universe. As players our job is to explore, make mistakes, fail, learn and grow. Mistakes are the magic of improv. Our flaws and faults lead us down paths that our conscious mind would never dare. An improv ensemble doesn't brace for the unknown, they embrace it. This is where the danger lives, where the fun is. The audience can feel us fearlessly playing with each other, with archetypes, and myth.

That is the improv mindset. In order to be an improviser and not a Control Freak, players must surrender to the ensemble, honor each other, and build a sense of togetherness and trust.

RUNT OF THE LITTER

In the early levels of an improv education, recreational players befriend the professional ones. As they develop, these differences become more obvious, especially when one player is always getting the same notes. Their attitude might be good. They are a team player, only they are consistently missing the point of the exercises, unintentionally stymying the group's progress.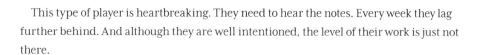

This type of player is heartbreaking. They need to hear the notes. Every week they lag further behind. And although they are well intentioned, the level of their work is just not there.

At the end of a rehearsal, address the difference in the room.

> INSTRUCTOR: *There is clearly a lot of love in the room for you as friends and teammates. We have grown to a point where there is disparity in talent and commitment in the room. As an instructor, I need to call this out for the health of the ensemble. I'd like to share what I see and then give you the week to think about how you'd like to proceed moving forward. Of course one option is to continue on as is but with the idea that I will start giving notes to individuals instead of giving the same notes to everyone. Another option is to see who wants to keep working and pushing and who wants this to be a fun drop-in environment. If a few of you would like to drop in, then we can save the last hour of every rehearsal for that, or we could have you join the rehearsal once every two to three weeks.*

This is a tough conversation, but necessary. It lets the ensemble know that you as instructor are aware of the team's unevenness and demonstrates that you are trying to balance it.

When this type of player takes things personally, it is an easier conversation to have.

> RUNT OF THE LITTER: *Everyone's moving so fast. It's confusing. I'm like, what's happening? Can we just slow down?*

If someone feels this way, then they should swim in a different lane. They may be outside of their talent pool, and they want to slow the ensemble down so that they can feel part of the fun. It's selfish but totally human.

They fear that their friends won't make time for them unless it is affiliated with improv. So they hang on tight, stunting the growth of the group and their friends. Let them go.

Ideally, this type of player is open to these notes and can feel the talent disparity in the room, in which case they can say,

> RUNT OF THE LITTER: *I love playing with you, but you are on a different level. I know that you need to grow, and I know that I'm holding you back. I will miss rehearsing with you, but we can still go to jams together.*

THE WALKING EXCUSE

Improv is hard and people don't like to fail. They will preemptively frame themselves with impediments to excuse their failings and short comings.

Don't expect GOOD work from me today because ...

... I'm exhausted. I'm sure I'm going to suck today.

... I'm hung over. Ignore anything I say. I feel like garbage.

... I've got a splitting headache. I can barely focus.

... I'm drowning in work. I'm probably going to be getting texts all class.

... I'm going through a break up. I can't right now.

Note this right away — If players enter the room already apologizing for not being one hundred percent present, give them an easy out. Don't waste the room's time with their excuses.

> INSTRUCTOR: *I don't want your attention to be split. If you're making apologies for yourself or your play in advance, it is unfair to your teammates. You can either leave now to go home rest, relax, and heal or address whatever's weighing on you and we will relay what was covered or you can sit and watch rehearsal without being a distraction.*

This sends a clear message that in rehearsals everyone is there to work. If they enter making excuses, then they are already bringing doubt into the room along with their lack of dedication. This stunts the ensemble with questions of commitment, connectivity and trust. The excuse is a crutch. It's a cry for attention. It makes ordinary work seem better than it is. Don't let players lower expectations so they can be applauded for doing the minimum. Excuses breed more excuses, weaving their way into the fabric and psyche of the group.

As a player, don't be a walking excuse of a teammate. If you're sick, text the group: *I feel sick. I don't want to get anyone else sick. I should go home and rest. Please let me know what you cover in class and how much I owe.* These are the words of a responsible adult.

Instructors must protect the sanctity of the rehearsal by keeping the players accountable and engaged. Of course, in the event major news springs up in the midst of rehearsal, give it the time, space and the attention it warrants.

THE STICKLER

On one hand, students want to express themselves and showcase their sense of humor. On the other, they want to align with the teacher's sensibilities and tick the boxes of their rubric. Straddling this line can be challenging. They may feel like they need to betray themselves and their instincts in order to gain favor of the teacher. The artist fights against the rules and parameters, while technical students obsess about doing everything to the letter, to the teacher's taste, striving for correctness.

A Level Two class hired me to help them perfect the Pattern Game. They insisted on running the pattern game over and over without scenes for three hours. When I made suggestions to help them be present and textured with their choices, they resisted.

>*That's not how we're supposed to do it.*

>*Our teacher wants it this way.*

>*We need to do it right for him, because he's the one grading us.*

If anyone tells you there is only one way to do improv, they are a zealot. Speaking in unbending dogmatic language is the language of tyrants and fossils. If the only reason we are making something is to impress someone else, then we may never be pleased ourselves.

Don't remove the self from your self-expression.

If we put all our self-worth into somebody else's hands, then what we make has very little to do with us. When you fail a class because you were following your instincts while taking the direction of the teacher, there's little to regret. But when you fail a class because you ignored your instincts to serve the teacher, there's nothing but regret.

THE WILD CARD

Wild Card players are agents of chaos, loose cannons that can run amok and throw curve balls at scenes from beyond left field. Some knowingly say things they'd never say in real life. They feel emboldened to be the most daring, weirdo versions of themself on stage. Others are unintentional Wild Cards based on who they are or how they see the world. Their vantage is skewed and every offer seems *out there*.

Help the Wild Card have self-restraint. Crazy stacked on crazy destroys realities. There's no sense. No horizon. The piece tailspins and the Wild Card panics and tries to fix the scene with more wildness because that's all they know.

Wild Cards get laughs easily, because they're weird. Don't let them rest on their randomness. Quick laughs stunt their growth and enforce bad habits. They don't need to grow a scene, or build a relationship to get a laugh, they can just enter and say anything.

Moderation is key. Scenes must be a dance. The ideal Wild Card knows that sometimes the owner walks the dog and sometimes the dog walks the owner. Wild choices need to be fenced in and managed before more wild choices can be added to a scene. They need to know when it's time to lead and when it's time to lose. This makes them aware and accountable as a teammate. The last thing we want is teammates bracing against their bizarreness.

FRUSTRATED TEAMMATE: *What's the point of building a scene if they're just going to knock it over?*

Unchecked Wild Card energy can become Wrecking Ball, energy destroying scenes and the spirt of ensemble. Most players take turns being the interesting or the interested. Teammates tire of always being the interested, always babysitting the Wild Card, mopping up after them, and in wriggles resentment.

> FRUSTRATED TEAMMATE: ***Why do we have to do all the heavy lifting? Why can't they do this for us?***

The instructor should stay a step ahead of these issues and correct behaviors before they get to a place of bitterness, where the ensemble surrenders, resigns to failure and stops doing any work.

Help the ensemble see the Wild Card for the treasure they are. Their presence introduces a coyote in the henhouse, creating drama and stakes. It gives everyone something to justify and rally around. The audience leans forward to see just how the team will make sense of these unpredictable choices.

Help the Wild Card understand their natural gift and use it thoughtfully, to accentuate the funny in others. Encourage them to play things real, and be normal and interested in other's interesting choices to grow as a performer and teammate.

If a team doesn't learn to embrace these players, delight in the weird, in the misinterpretations of aphorisms or normal parts of speech taken literally, they become a scapegoat.

> *If not for this person, we'd have done a good show.*

> *If not for this person, we could actually get somewhere in rehearsals.*

> *If not for this person, we'd be so much better.*

Take ownership. Instead of pointing fingers at others, take accountability for yourself. How can you be better? How can you make others better? How can you lift them up? When we blame others, we're hemorrhaging energy instead of putting in the work.

TYPES OF INSTRUCTORS

THE BRAGGART

The Braggart is a stage hog and narcissist. They love getting paid to hang out and be themselves. Rehearsals meander away from the work. The spotlight shifts from the ensemble to the instructor who regales their Super Fans with stories of cool moves they've made in the past, or what it was like on the set of some TV show. Rehearsal time is gone in a blink along with all your money.

If your teacher makes a habit of showing up late and looks for any moment to monologue and steal focus, address them. Ask them to stay on task.

People don't speak up out of fear of making enemies with the coach, or hurting their feelings and then having them hold a grudge. But there is nothing wrong with advocating for better time management. You're not being mean; you are being responsible with your time.

If the teacher ignores your request, then it is time to reassess why you're trusting them to guide you as an improv team. Call a team meeting and get a read of the room. If the majority is a bunch of fanboys, then maybe they're perfectly happy with the instructor and maybe this means you should adjust your agenda or leave the group. If the group shares your sentiment, kindly let the coach know.

> STUDENTS: *We want to be well-rounded players and although we've loved working with you we feel we should rotate to a new coach for a different perspective. We'd like to spend the last two weeks with you getting as much done as possible and who knows? Maybe we can circle back in the future.*

THE CHEERLEADER

The Cheerleader cares more about morale than pushing the art form.

> CHEERLEADER: *Great job!! That was awesome!! Ya'll are killing it.*

They find a bright side in everything, wanting everybody to feel good about themselves and the way they're playing. This is an inspiring quality for a coach to have, but it should not be the only quality they have.

They need to note effectively, think critically, and rectify what's wrong with scenes. Otherwise, you are paying them to be your biggest fan. Under their watch, the ensemble gets reps and experience but little guidance. An instructor should encourage and challenge you to be your best.

Often the cheerleader doesn't have a critical eye, so they make sweeping statements.

Great job!!

Why was it a great job?
Because it was awesome!!

Why was it awesome?
Because Improv's magic like that.

These reasons are fluff, so sunny you can't see any substance in what they are saying. Their applause and praise are a smokescreen. And it's nearly impossible for newer players to look past the laughs and compliments to question its validity and value. They'd prefer to believe the hype whether it's real or not. This gives students a false sense of security in their talent, progress and performance.

If the whole team thrives off this positivity, wonderful. Keep the instructor, but recognize you are not getting notes, and that bad habits will be reinforced just as much as the good ones.

If the majority of the team feels they want more, ask for critical notes, personal notes, overarching team notes, side coaching. If they don't have any input, it's time to move on. If you'd still like to continue with them, supply them with an aim for the group.

Call out when we drop our object work.
Underline when we negate each other.
Push us to make more active choices.

This is more than students should have to do. Rethink why you are paying this instructor for their services.

THE SNAKE OIL SALESMAN

This type of instructor had one or two years training at a notable improv school such as iO, Second City, UCB, etc. They then moved to a smaller market city where there may not even be an improv scene. They launch a MeetUp group and share lessons they learned. People are amazed that they studied at the same school as Tina Fey or Steve Carrell. *Oh my God, you performed there? You're incredible. Please teach us!* So they do. As the adoration and trust in the instructor builds, soon they are revered for their **experience**. The community starts revolving around their teaching even though they only have a slight head start on their students.

Imagine a sculptor, a dentist, or a ski instructor — would you trust them to guide you, to work on your teeth, or get safely down a black diamond with less than a week's worth of experience? No. But with improv it's all ethereal. Instructors are as great as they say they are, and when people adopt their measuring stick to measure themselves, it's easy to become the gold standard, a guru, an authority.

These instructors start believing their own illusion, stealing your time, taking your trust.

Question these types of leaders.
Is the system growing?
Is it healthy?
Do they get results?
When they invite guest instructors in, do they allow themselves to be changed?
Are they malleable?
Are they afraid to be a student in front of the other students?
Are they threatened or excited by new ideas?
Do they discredit outside influences or welcome them?
Do they prefer group knowledge or their own authority?

> **Side Note:** As an instructor, don't be a snake oil salesman. From the start, admit that you are a relative novice and explain that you only have a slight head start from the few classes you took. Profess that you have a lot to learn, but that you are willing to share what you can with the community. Don't mislead them. The more you posture and pose to be an expert, the more you will stress to keep up that facade. You'll fear your students finding out that you're a fraud. Put your energy in growing together, not in putting on airs.

When an instructor's knowledge base and skill set are stunted, the students and community will also be stunted.

The best thing an instructor like this can do for their community is offer a JOY OF IMPROV class, sharing whatever exercises and techniques they gleaned from the instruction they had. Drill these exercises for reps, keep the notes minimal and participate as a peer not an expert. If this instructor truly cares about growing the culture, they should be inviting renowned guest instructors with more than five thousand hours of teaching experience to work with everyone. This builds the improv savvy of the community.

Next, encourage students to travel, taking intensives as explorers and ambassadors, attending festivals, making connections, taking detailed notes, with the aim of sharing them with the community at large.

If this section rings true to you as an instructor, be kind to yourself. You fell into this role for very human reasons. It is never too late to be honest, call a meeting and shoot it straight. Explain that you have little more experience than everyone else but that you do love the art form and the community, so you want to share the power and allow everyone to steer where they'd like to take this art form in order to create a healthy balanced system.

THE TOUGH TEACHER

The Tough Teacher revels in being needlessly cruel. They lay into students. They rip good and bad scenes to shreds and laugh at the group, as opposed to with it. Rubbing a team's faces in their mistake mainly builds shame. A good instructor helps you learn through failure, instead of rejoicing in your failure.

There is a time for brutally hard notes, but an instructor must provide scaffolding to handle the weight of those notes. Don't pay to be bogged down by their negativity. They should be kind and honest.

However, certain improvisers gravitate to this type. They pride themselves on studying with merciless hard asses. This type of student is usually a theoretical improviser, who doesn't actually like doing improv as much as talking shop and theory about improv.

Don't make excuses for this type of teacher. Their bitterness will only blacken the psyche of the team.

> STUDENTS: *We appreciate your notes and expertise. But week after week, we feel like we're letting you down because after all these months working with you we're still getting the same notes. At the end of this month we're going to shift to someone else, regroup and go back to basics.*

THE MONEY EATERS

Teaching improv is a beautiful thing that we cheapen with a price tag. Certain students flock to instructors who set insanely high rates. They associate price with prestige and expertise.

What is value?
What are we paying for?
What does the instructor provide?

A high-priced instructor indirectly stratifies the improv community into classes, not by talent, or drive, or potential but by finances, those who can and can't afford their classes.

The audacity of a single teacher over-reaching emboldens others to raise their prices. These instructors become improv world-eaters, flying into towns demanding hotels and pre-show hummus and Red Bulls. And the more we cater to their every whim, the more diva-like they become. When they leave town, the community is dirt broke. They can't afford to keep rehearsing because they blew their budget feeding an instructor's bank account and ego. They go into hibernation mode until players have the funds to start up again.

Often people will convince themselves that they made a good investment by bringing an instructor in because they don't want to admit they wasted their money. Be honest with yourself — was the instructor expensive and not all that impactful? If they were, don't bring them back.

Improv should be about exchanging ideas and creativity. The real currency is in connection and celebration. Be a compassionate instructor. Invest in the communities that are eager to learn from you. Get inventive match every overpriced class taught to the wealthy, with the same workshop taught to a marginalized community for free, or designate eight slots at the high price point and eight slots at a discount to ensure socio-economic diversity within the class.

PERFECTIONIST

This type of instructor is always on time, and ready to work. They game plan for rehearsals, communicate clearly and provide constructive notes. They take pride in their preparedness and the team's work. However, their pursuit of perfection exceeds the group's drive and ambition and sucks the fun out of the room.

If the instructor's engine burns with the power of a thousand suns, students will always feel dim by comparison. Unrealistic goals wear on a team. Chasing after the perfect piece can be exhausting, like running on a Möbius strip treadmill with no end, and no sense of accomplishment or satisfaction or growth. All the work starts to feel worthless and can break the team's spirit.

Students are ashamed and reluctant to voice their concerns. They are thinking, *How dare we ask this person to root and care and champion us less?*

The instructor is there to promote the ensemble, not induce guilt in the team. If your team is working with this type of instructor, help them see the importance of mini-victories.

> Students: *We love having you in our corner. You push us to get better and care more than we even care sometimes. But we talked and feel this dynamic needs to find a better balance. Your experience and passion set expectations and goals that seem beyond us. As a result, it's hard to feel proud of all the progress we've made with you. We'd like to set benchmarks for ourselves and truly celebrate when we surpass them.*

This acknowledges their dedication and professionalism while resetting the pace and aims for the ensemble to rebalance the team/coach dynamic.

THE WELL ROUNDED INSTRUCTOR

An improv teacher is part coach, part expert, part artist and part psychologist. They are a gardener attentively weeding the psyche of the group, always assessing what the group needs and how much they need it. They should know when to push and when to cradle. They create a celebratory culture of agreement and inspiration so that offers are heard and buoyed up. A great teacher does not just teach to their taste and vision but can see a student's intentions and align with them, refining them so that they can be as clear as possible.

The best type of instructor will have a healthy balance of these qualities. They know their worth. They are encouraging. They have confidence but don't need everything to be about them. They have a critical eye and a curious mind. They have a gift for giving constructive criticism, and they can see reasons to celebrate the good work and applaud the bravery to fail, while still pushing the ensemble to get better.

As well-rounded instructors we understand that progress is a process. We share what we love about the art form. We believe improv can inspire and elicit change, push boundaries, break down doors, hold a mirror up to society and offer commentary with unflinching truth. We empower every student to be better listeners, better teammates, better partners, and more connected to their emotions. We help players to embrace the unknown, break out of their ruts, and liberate themselves from themselves to play in a state of flow. We are patient. We are kind.

We are communicative. We take pride in coaching. We champion a teams' growth with pointed personal notes. We come to rehearsals remembering where we left off and raring to go. We have a game plan, and a heart, and are able to phrase notes so everyone understands the lesson. We value brilliance and theatricality and help bring awareness and equity. We unlock imagination, cultivate self-confidence, and nurture collaboration within the team and within each player, so that their internal musician and technician can work in concert. The internal critic can applaud the artist self, and the artist can be open to and not broken by tweaks, notes and polish. We rein in egos, balancing the interested and interesting.

We value each person's voice, vantage, justifications, insights and instincts, offers and gifts. We are open and interested in connecting with people and ideas. We empower students to innovate and are excited by their innovations, not intimidated. We create a space to fail, laugh and learn. We shine a light on each student to help them bloom. And when they're stuck inside their thoughts we are there, ready, with a purple marker to scribble across the page.

EPILOGUE

My father passed on January 9th, 2021. He was surrounded by his loving family in his former Rochester home. He battled cancer with grit and grace, making every minute count, spending time with loved ones, and finishing every project possible. It was an honor and privilege to provide for a man who provided so much to me. He instilled in me the importance of bringing excellence and pride into everything you do. He turned my Constructs into moats and bridges and horse stables for my sister's *My Little Ponies*. He used in-camera special effects to abracadabra a plastic Fischer-Price Magic Kit into actual magic and made me believe I could do anything I could imagine. He helped unlock my imagination through his own creativity and genius. He showed me determination and what it is to work. He taught me to appreciate design and intentionality. He showed me how to fail and not fear it, and how to look for lessons in everything. He had vision, passion, and MacGyver-like resourcefulness. He showed me the world, gave me his love, taught me tenacity, shared his knowledge, wisdom and laughter, and most of all his friendship. I may never be a dad, but I learned how to be a great one from his example. Some of my most cherished memories were spending time with him, whether it was riding south on a train from Venice to Florence while he double-fisted tiny bottles of wine; sitting and laughing out back on his patio in Puerto Rico; eating razor clams in Barcelona; or simply letting me dunk my buttered toast in his coffee. He helped me chase my dreams and wrangle them. He made his mark on the world in everything he did, not just in what he made, but how he made it. He was a craftsman who never half-assed anything. He always looked to leave the world in better shape than he found it. I was always in awe in the wake of his genius and love. He underlined things that begged to be appreciated in the world, in people, and in nature. He has given me so much. He sacrificed so that I could stand on his shoulders to see the world from a better vantage. I am blessed and thankful to be his son.

Months after he passed, family and friends would call and tell me when he'd come to them in their dreams. I know he and I had said everything we needed to say to each other, but still, I wanted to see him again. Then early one morning, in Bremen, Germany, I woke up before my alarm, then went back to sleep. All of a sudden, I was at New York Pizza Suprema, near Penn Station. I ordered and they told me to sit and for some reason, they slid me a ticket and said to listen for my number like it was a DMV. People were sitting staggered diagonally from each other at different booths, waiting. When I sat down I looked up and to my right was my dad. We just started grabbing for each other's arms, to know that we were real, and he felt solid and we laughed. I didn't know how it was happening. I was just so happy to see him. And I said, **Who'd have thought that heaven would be a DMV Pizza Shop?** and he said, **I don't think I'm in heaven.** And then we laughed more, just holding each other's forearms. I told him I loved him, that I miss him and that I think about him every day. Then I said, **I guess if I ever miss you I just have to go to a DMV or come to this pizza shop.** And then he said **Or you can just laugh.** Then I woke up. It had only been two minutes, but it was so much more.

I love getting to work with people. I love being on stage. I love helping teams hear, listen, endorse, and celebrate each other's choices, to create something greater than themselves. I get to travel the world and laugh. And every time I do, I can hear my father laughing along. It's a little slice of heaven. The greatest way to honor him is to do the things that I love, to bring love into everything I do, to inspire communities to try new things and not fear failing, to learn and grow with each other, and collaborate to make great things with craft, care and love.

Made in United States
Orlando, FL
04 December 2024

54977332R00122